PALMERTOWN
PRESS

La Porte City, Iowa

Copyright © 2024 by Michael Whittlesey

ISBN 978-1-7320800-4-1

Mary & Bob Whittlesey, 2001

Cliff & Nancy McFarland, 2008

This book is dedicated to Robert and Mary Whittlesey and Clifford and Nancy McFarland. While the Honor Flight program (and this book) pays tribute to the brave men and women who have served their country, such service comes at a cost for the family members who support their loved ones stationed near and far away. While Bob, with the U.S. Air Force, and Cliff, with the U.S. Navy, were serving their nation honorably domestically and abroad, Mary and Nancy were selflessly supporting their efforts at home. It takes all kinds of service to keep a nation, and a family, safe. I am grateful for both. ~MW

Contents

Foreward

In May 2011, the call came just days before the second Honor Flight originating from Waterloo, Iowa would lift off, sending more than 90 Eastern Iowa veterans on a trip of a lifetime to Washington, D.C.. Due to an unfortunate circumstance, a vacancy had created an open seat on the airplane. As the Editor and Publisher of *The Progress Review*, the weekly newspaper based in nearby La Porte City, I was asked if I would be interested in covering the event. With four local veterans, the first from La Porte City to be included in an Honor Flight originating from Waterloo, of course I was very interested. That I had never before been to the nation's capital helped seal the deal.

Loaded up with a bevy of cameras and equipment, I boarded the plane, determined to capture and record as much of the day as possible. When I returned home that night, I was surprised to discover I had taken well over 600 photos and had shot nearly an hour of video footage. Of course, the best photos I had of the four local veterans made their way onto the front page of the next edition of *The Progress Review*. But what to do with the other images? They certainly illustrated the incredible experience in ways far better than any words I could write.

Because *The Progress Review* was very much a family owned and operated business, my wife, Jane, and I discussed at length what could be done with the rich material we had stored on various camera cards. Using my experience creating short video programs, I fired up my video editing software and began adding photos and music until I was satisfied with a slide show that presented images of the Honor Flight experience from lift-off to the return celebration in Waterloo. A second presentation was created in a similar fashion, this time with the video footage.

Having been rewarded with an incredible trip to Washington, D.C., I was ready to repay the Cedar Valley Honor Flight Board's invitation to cover the event with a proposal of my own. If they were satisfied with the quality of the programs I had created, we would use them to create a commemorative DVD that would be shipped to each veteran,

free of charge. After meeting with several board members and receiving the go-ahead, we did just that.

Following that initial mailing, something amazing happened. Veterans, wanting extra copies of the DVD for their guardians and family members, began asking how they could get more of them.

Honor Flights may be many things for the veterans who enjoy them, but one thing they are not is cheap. With each flight costing more than $100,000, the Cedar Valley Honor Flight hub has had to raise more than $3 million to support their volunteer efforts over a 14 year period of time.

As much as we were pleased by the response to the DVD, we hadn't considered the possibility of distributing them to anyone else. Because of the costs associated with each flight, Jane and I were in agreement that such an effort should benefit Cedar Valley Honor Flight in some way. At a subsequent meeting with the board, we agreed to produce additional DVDs for the general public and return all proceeds from their sales to support future Cedar Valley Honor Flights.

At the time, we had no way of knowing that our working relationship with Cedar Valley Honor Flight was just beginning. We just knew that something very special was being done for Eastern Iowa veterans and wanted to help any way we could. Using our skills to produce commemorative DVDs seemed like a natural way to honor each of our fathers, both who had served in the U.S. military, and to show our support for the veteran community.

When the third Cedar Valley Honor Flight was preparing to lift off in September 2011, we were pleased to receive the invitation to send another person along. Truth be told, Jane is a far better photographer than I'll ever hope to be, so on this trip she did the honors. A second batch of DVDs soon followed, this time with a handy order form to streamline the reorder process.

Over the years, our involvement covering Cedar Valley Honor Flight has continued, even after *The Progress Review* ceased publication in 2020. During this time, we have been grateful for the assistance

from other photographers who provided coverage for us when we were not present on scheduled flights. Thanks to Mary Bauer, John Klotzbach and Katie Davison, we have been able to provide commemorative DVDs for nearly 3,000 Cedar Valley Honor Flight veterans, spanning 28 consecutive flights.

The idea for this book began to percolate as our assortment of Honor Flight photographs had grown to nearly 10,000 images. Showcasing some of the very best photos from our collection, the images contained on the pages of this book begin to explain why a committed group of volunteers continue their fund-raising efforts to honor area veterans. The rest of the story is revealed by way of commentary and quotes gathered following a series of interviews with the volunteers who remain engaged in what can only be described as a labor of love.

The story of Cedar Valley Honor Flight is a photographic journey that illustrates how a grateful community honors the men and women who put their country before themselves. It's a story about the importance of what it means to serve others.

As part of this journey, a certain amount of context is needed to fully appreciate what a wonderful experience it is to spend a day in Washington, D.C. with a group of veterans. You'll find that context in the form of newspaper columns I wrote back in the day, as well as summaries that provide some of the history and interesting facts about the monuments and memorials we have visited along the way.

Reflecting on the images contained on these pages, I am filled with gratitude for the veterans who have served our great nation. I am also thankful for the service of the Cedar Valley Honor Flight volunteers who have devoted so much time and effort to acknowledge area veterans in this very special way.

I hope you, dear reader, enjoy the journey as much as I have enjoyed compiling it.

-Mike Whittlesey
January 2024

Cedar Valley Honor Flight Story

"THANK YOU FOR YOUR SERVICE!"

The Birth of a National Network

When the World War II Memorial was dedicated in Washington, D.C. on May 29, 2004, it quickly became a topic of conversation for retired Air Force Captain and physician's assistant, Earl Morse, and his patients. Morse had been hired by the Department of Veterans Affairs six years prior to work in a small health clinic in Springfield, Ohio, and was eager to learn if the members of the Greatest Generation he served were planning to travel to the nation's capital to visit the memorial built specifically to honor them. Over time, it became clear to him that, for most of the veterans, now living in their 80's, such a trip was not physically or financially possible.

Undeterred, Morse, who was also a private pilot and member of one of the largest aero clubs located at Wright-Patterson Air Force Base in Dayton, Ohio, conceived a plan to take matters into his own hands. In December 2004, he asked two of his veteran patients if they would be willing to make the trip to Washington, D.C. if Morse personally flew them, free of charge. The response he got from both, tears followed by eager acceptance, confirmed his belief that there were many veterans who, like them, would feel the same way.

In January 2005, Morse took the idea to his aero club, describing a volunteer program consisting of two requirements. The first, a free trip for the veterans, meant that pilots would pay the cost of the aircraft rental (up to $1,200 for the day). The second was the stipulation that the pilots would also personally escort the veterans around the nation's capital to complete the experience. Following his presentation, eleven pilots immediately expressed their desire to participate.

Four months later, in May 2005, six small planes and 12 veterans landed in Manassas, Virginia, before boarding vans that transported the group to the World War II Memorial. Word of this incredible experience soon spread. With so many veterans wanting to participate, commercial aircraft were used to transport up to 40 veterans at a time, many of them in wheelchairs. By the end of 2005, 137 World War II veterans had made the trip to Washington, D.C..

A growing waiting list and an urgent desire to serve an aging population of seniors before they died saw an increase of veterans served in 2006. By that time, news of the volunteer effort was spreading across the nation and a network of community leaders who shared

a mission and vision of what the Honor Flight program could be was coming together.

In Hendersonville, North Carolina, Jeff Miller was the first to organize and obtain the necessary funding to do what was considered impossible; fly an entire commercial jet filled with World War II veterans and their guardians to Washington, D.C.. It was also during this time that Morse and Miller combined their efforts, co-founding the Honor Flight Network. By the end of 2006, nearly 900 World War II veterans had visited their memorial in Washington, D.C., courtesy of this life-changing program.

By the end of 2022, the Honor Flight Network had expanded to include more than 130 hubs located across 45 states, adding Korean and Vietnam War era veterans to their service mission. Because of the efforts of thousands of dedicated volunteers, more than 270,000 United States veterans have received grateful thanks for their service by way of an unforgettable experience in Washington, D.C..

Creating a Hub in Waterloo, Iowa

In Eastern Iowa, a similar story began with a simple conversation in 2010 between Black Hawk County Supervisor, Craig White, and local media mogul, Jim Coloff, about potential projects that could benefit the military veterans in and around the Waterloo-Cedar Falls community.

Coloff, who owns a dozen Iowa radio stations and is well known for his charitable work giving back to the communities he serves, was looking to develop a project for area veterans. Who better to call than the man affectionately known as "Whitey," an army veteran with countless family members who have proudly served their country for generations in the various branches of the United States military? As the men met sporadically for coffee to brainstorm ideas over the next few months, their early conversations did not generate any particular course of action. It wasn't until White read about an Honor Flight experience in the *Waterloo Courier* originating out of nearby Cedar Rapids, that the idea to serve local veterans in the same capacity began to take hold.

An informational meeting to learn more about the Cedar Rapids Honor Flight operation was soon set. Joining White for the meeting was fellow Black Hawk County Supervisor, Frank Magsamen, who had expressed an interest in helping with any project that might benefit local veterans. Magsamen brought with him a lifetime of service devoted to the local fire department, rising through the ranks to become Fire Chief in 1994, before ultimately serving as the Emergency Management Director for Black Hawk County.

Following the meeting, the two supervisors immediately recognized the Honor Flight experience as a good cause but were taken aback by the amount of money needed to make it work. Each flight came with a price tag in excess of $100,000.

"The amount of money was the thing that scared me because I'd never been involved with anything to raise that kind of money," White recalled.

"When I left Cedar Rapids, I thought what a responsibility it is to take 80-90 World War II veterans and coordinate to get an airplane here. I was pretty much overwhelmed about it," Magsamen added.

Uncertain how they could proceed in the face of such a massive fund-raising campaign, fate would intervene by way of a lost phone number. In an effort to reach him, White's Cedar Rapids Honor Flight contact instead called *Waterloo Courier* reporter, Pat Kinney, when he discovered he had misplaced White's phone number. As any good reporter will do, Kinney began asking questions about possible Honor Flights taking off from Waterloo. After White responded that additional planning was needed before he could say much about it, the next day he was surprised to see a report in the *Courier* about the effort underway for Waterloo to host an Honor Flight. With this "announcement" going public, there would be no turning back now.

While White may have initially thought the *Courier's* story to be premature, it served the purpose of reinvigorating efforts to find the money to make the dream of making Waterloo, Iowa an Honor Flight hub into a reality. Unbeknownst to White and Magsamen, that same story had gotten others in the community to begin thinking similar thoughts.

A Remarkable Gift Pays it Forward

Burk "Skeet" Miehe is the founder of American Pattern and CNC Works, Inc., a company that serves production pattern tooling needs for agricultural and industrial businesses. His father was a Marine who had served in the Korean War, a member of the "Frozen Chosen," so named for an extended battle fought during the worst blizzard in a century at the Chosin Reservoir in North Korea. His wife, Julie, also shares a special military connection, as her father was a U.S. Navy pilot.

Burk has known Craig White for many years, dating back to their time playing softball together in the 1980s. When White paid him a visit to seek support from his business, he was aware of the outreach effort the fledgling Honor Flight hub was making.

"He had gone around to some other business leaders and was trying to raise some money and they weren't having a lot of luck," he recalled.

As the two began to discuss the Honor Flight program, little did Craig White know he was about to receive a gift that would more than jump-start his fund-raising campaign.

"When Des Moines, Mason City and Cedar Rapids [have Honor Flights, and here's Waterloo [without one]... I just felt, yeah, we've got to do something to help. There's a lot of veterans in this area," Miehe said.

White looked on as Miehe got out his checkbook, started the dollar amount with the number one, then proceeded to add five zeroes after it. With a single stroke of Burk's pen, the Miehes had funded the entire cost of Cedar Valley Honor Flight's inaugural trip to Washington, D.C..

"I think they were shocked," Miehe said when asked about the response he got.

"We [the business] had a very good 2009 and 2010. And this was 2011. And I felt, why not? Why not pay it back?"

Waterloo, Iowa

The Cedar Valley Honor Flight logo proudly shares its name with American Legion Post 730 in Waterloo, Iowa: Sullivan-Hartogh-Davis. These three names represent the ultimate sacrifice seven Waterloo natives made in the service of their nation.

The five Sullivan brothers- George (age 27), Frank (25), Joe (23), Matt (22) and Al (19) enlisted in the United States Navy on January 3, 1942, during World War II, following the death of their sister's boyfriend, who was killed while serving on the *USS Arizona* during the Japanese attack on Pearl Harbor. While siblings were not typically allowed to serve together during wartime, the Sullivans requested and received permission from the Secretary of the Navy to do so. Assigned to the *USS Juneau*, all five were killed when their ship was struck by a Japanese submarine's torpedo on November 13, 1942, and sank near the Solomon Islands in the South Pacific Ocean.

Nearly twenty-seven years later, Marine Lance Corporal David Michael Hartogh was killed just three days after his 19th birthday on September 7, 1969 in the Quang Nam Province of South Vietnam.

A seventh Waterloo serviceman, Marine Private First Class David Lee Davis, was killed less than two months after his 19th birthday on March 20, 1969, as part of Operation Purple Martin, a multi-battalion search and clear operation in the Quang Tri Province of South Vietnam.

These seven men, whose names are honored by American Legion Post 730 and Cedar Valley Honor Flight, share important legacies that, to this day, remain in the hearts and minds of the Waterloo community. Their service and sacrifice remind future generations that our nation remains free because of their patriotism and acts of selflessness.

"Certainly, the Miehe's donation got the community looking at doing the flights out of Waterloo. He got the flights going," Magsamen acknowledged, recalling how the impact of such a tremendous gift encouraged other businesses and the community at large to follow suit.

Building a Team

With the knowledge that at least one flight was now possible, there was still much work to be done to build the new Waterloo Honor Flight hub from the ground up. White and Magsamen knew they needed help from a number of volunteers to help make their vision of Cedar Valley Honor Flight a reality. What to do first?

"A bunch of paperwork," White said with a chuckle.

And who got the unenviable task of completing the documentation for the organization to obtain its necessary nonprofit status?

"I think Frank filled out most of it," he added.

"At that time, you could be a 501(c)(3) through the National Honor Flight, so that's how we got our initial start," Magsamen explained.

To solicit volunteer support, a meeting at the local United Auto Workers 838 hall was scheduled and promoted by the *Waterloo Courier* in a news article that described some of the desired skills and abilities that were being sought. A number of individuals who would become key contributors in the Cedar Valley Honor Flight organization took notice, and soon, the roster of board members began to take shape.

Thank You for Your Service

Waterloo, Iowa

On early support for Cedar Valley Honor Flight:

"I just felt we've got to do something to help. There's a lot of veterans in this area. And I felt, why not? Why not pay it back?"

~Burk Miehe, Business Owner

Among them was Janet Liming, who, despite already having a full-time job, shared a passion for the veteran community, having a father who had served as a medic in the army and a son who served in the Marine Corps.

"I had seen in the news that they were looking for people to serve on the board to assist. So I went to the meeting, and I had sent an e-mail to Craig that said these are my qualifications and I would love to do this. I became the first administrator [for Cedar Valley Honor Flight] and what that involved was quite a bit more than I ever imagined. But I never, ever say it wasn't one of the best things in the world. It was the most rewarding thing I've ever done in my life," she said.

Lee Bedore, following a 37 year career working in all aspects of the John Deere foundry, machining and assembly, spoke with fellow Deere retiree Craig White about the effort to establish an Honor Flight hub in Waterloo. Bedore, who was the Chair of Community Services at UAW Local 838 for nearly 30 years, had been active serving the community on a number of different boards for years.

"It's just another way to give back to Waterloo and it's time to help out. I'm very appreciative of the vets," he said of his interest in the project. "I talked to Craig and they needed a place to meet. The Union hall seemed to work out. [It's been] a great place to have our meetings at," he added.

Also, stepping up to volunteer for the first Honor Flight was David Grimm, a 33 year veteran of the United States armed forces, having served in both the Marine Corps and Army. His first role as parking attendant at pre-flight meetings and the airport soon morphed into other logistical tasks for the organization.

"I used to drive down to Cedar Rapids and pick up wheelchairs from [Eastern Iowa] Honor Flight, bring them up here. I would take them back down afterwards," he said.

Sue Gress was a volunteer and publisher of two cookbooks for Iowa's Bravest, an organization that supports Iowa servicemen and women while they are deployed overseas, when she learned about Waterloo's effort to establish an Honor Flight hub. Following the example set by her parents, who proudly served their country in the U.S. Army, Sue had four brothers who served in various branches of the military, as well as a son in the Marine Corps. Thanks to her calligraphy skills, a touch of elegance was added to the table place cards used at pre-flight meetings and the lanyards worn on Honor Flight trips. Like so many other Cedar Valley Honor Flight veterans, she's pitched in wherever needed, be it making phone calls, helping serve meals or checking veterans in at the airport

"I wanted to give back to the veterans. I just felt that was so important," she said.

Before serving Cedar Valley Honor Flight, Ed McFarland served his country a total of eight years in the U.S. Army and National Guard. His interest in the organization was sparked after being a guardian on the first flight in May 2011.

"I just felt as a younger vet that it would be an honor to be able to go out to D.C. with these older vets and get to hear some of their stories. And then, when I got back, it meant a lot to me to be able to go out there. I told Craig White if they ever needed help to let me know," McFarland recalled.

Soon, he was put to work helping prepare for the pre-flight meetings before joining the board and getting involved with fund-raising work.

From the very beginning, Cedar Valley Honor Flight also received support from another key business partner, the local Hy-Vee grocery stores. With the assistance of Niki Rinaldi, who served on the Cedar Valley Honor Flight Board for several years, Hy-Vee has provided an immense amount of support in the form of meals for every veteran and guardian attending pre-flight meetings (29 and counting by the end

of 2023). They also sponsored donuts, fruit and coffee at the Waterloo Regional Airport on the mornings of each flight. Early flights also featured a Hy-Vee "goody bag" for veterans, each containing snacks and a disposable camera loaded with film that the grocery store chain processed for free.

Starting from Scratch

With volunteers ready and willing to work, procedures needed to be developed to streamline the process of selecting and transporting veterans to Washington, D.C.. With no personal experience to draw upon, the small but eager Cedar Valley Honor Flight Board consulted with another area Honor Flight hub, Eastern Iowa Honor Flight, which serves veterans in nearby Cedar Rapids.

"I met with a gal named Mary in Cedar Rapids who was an administrator. She showed me all the paperwork [Cedar Rapids used] and gave me a rundown of everything that had to be done. So I came home and created our own paperwork," Janet Liming recalled.

Teresa Schmitz, another volunteer who made an early commitment to Cedar Valley Honor Flight, also found the consultation in Cedar Rapids to be very helpful.

"We learned how important it was to look through the files [and check] the medical needs of our guys," she said, emphasizing the special care that was taken for World War II veterans, most of whom were in their 80s and 90s.

Forms that had to be adapted for the Waterloo hub included applications for veterans and guardians to complete. An all-important medical information sheet was needed so that any prescribed medications or other special medical needs, such as oxygen, could be reported and accounted for. A covenant not

to sue form was also adapted for use with veterans and guardians flying out of Waterloo.

Early flights, which featured veterans of World War II and the Korean War, posed unique challenges.

"I think the World War II veterans, hardly any of them had been to see any of the memorials. So, for them, this was huge. Plus, a lot of them probably had never been on a plane. But as far as health-wise, it was more challenging with the World War II veterans because of their age, the amount of oxygen needed and medications," said longtme volunteer, Barb O'Rourke.

With applications available at a number of locations in and around Waterloo, as well as online, the response from World War II and Korean War veterans to the early Cedar Valley Honor Flights was very strong.

"At that time, we were getting so many applications that we had to be really, really careful [to record] the date that we received them," O'Rourke said, because veterans receiving their confirmation card paid close attention to the confirmed date their application was received.

Once applications have been submitted, a follow-up phone call is needed to confirm eligibility, that the veteran is available to go on the scheduled flight date and to determine if any special accommodations are needed. Over the years, these calls have been made by a number of volunteers, including Janet Liming, Linda Bergmann, Sue Gress, Barb O'Rourke, Teresa Schmitz and Janet Schupbach.

"We have to get [the veteran's] information, birthdate and everything else like that so it will match up with the manifest," Schupbach stated, referencing the importance of accuracy, as the plane's manifest must match each individual's

Thank You for Your Service

Sullivan ★ Hartogh ★ Davis
Cedar Valley
Honor Flight
Waterloo
Waterloo, Iowa

On why he volunteered for Cedar Valley Honor Flight:

"I belong to just about every military organization there is. As a veteran myself, I saw how we were treated. I thought it was a great thing to pay it forward and pay it back. I'm happy to do it and it's an honor to do it."

~David Grimm, Honor Flight Organizer

identification on the day of the flight in order for them to travel with the group.

Bergman, who has served as flight administrator for nearly 25 flights, said the phone calls also serve as an opportunity for veterans to get excited about the upcoming trip.

"We always try to get excited for them. [I'll say] 'Hi, this is Linda with Honor Flight and this is your lucky day. I'm calling to see if you want to go with us.'"

Janet Liming recalled a time when the call she placed was answered by a woman whose tone soon changed when she learned who was calling.

"[When] I said this is Janet with the Honor Flight, her tone totally changed. She's yelling for her husband, 'Dear, dear! Come to the phone! It's the Honor Flight.'"

During that call, veterans are also asked if they have someone in mind who will serve as their guardian. Guardians are considered essential for the success of the Honor Flight mission, as they help ensure that every veteran has a safe and memorable experience. Depending on a veteran's needs, a guardian may be assigned to assist more than one veteran making the trip. Though Honor Flights provide veterans with a free trip to Washington, D.C., each guardian must pay for the privilege to travel. For Cedar Valley Honor Flight guardians, that cost could be $600 or more.

With each Cedar Valley Honor Flight, organizers plan their manifest with the number of 165 passengers in mind. That represents the maximum number of veterans, guardians,

media members and support personnel, such as doctors, nurses and emergency medical technicians, that the airplane can accommodate. Organizers must be ever vigilant of that number as they confirm veteran eligibility and make guardian assignments, for things can change very quickly.

"People will call and say, 'Oh I guess we can't go.' So we pull them out and get somebody else in there. So it's constant troubleshooting," Linda Bergmann noted. "I remember it was probably the third time I took a flight. I called Barb [O'Rourke] and I said,'I'm gonna get fired. I've got five too many people on the flight. She said, 'It'll be fine. You'll see, somebody will cancel.' The next day, a veteran and his guardian couldn't go. So that knocked it down to three. Then one of my three medical people couldn't go," she recalled.

The situation resolved itself because Cedar Valley Honor Flight tries to assign at least two people to "standby" status, making them available for travel in the event of a last minute cancellation.

"I try to get a veteran and guardian [available for standby] so that if a group cancels, you can slide them right in. Most of them are very willing to do that," Bergmann said, explaining that it is rare when people who are at the airport as a standby do not get to make the trip that day.

While selecting and preparing 165 people to safely spend a day in the nation's capital is a monumental task, it is only part of the Honor Flight equation. There are travel plans that must be made. Decisions regarding the

Honor Flight date must be made. A contract for the airline providing the charter service must be completed. Likewise, once the plane is on the ground, three charter buses must be ready to provide ground transportation. While in Washington, D.C., lunch and dinner service must be provided for a party of 165 people.

Fortunately for Honor Flight hubs, the national organization offers assistance with these travel arrangements. Still, there must be someone locally to confirm those arrangements are in place before the plane lifts off the ground. Looking back, Frank Magsamen, the person his fellow board members credit for initially making it happen, admitted that work that once seemed overwhelming eventually became manageable:

"Just kind of piece by piece, it came together. We figured out how to do the charters out there- everything, [including] the buses and the meals," he said.

"We've done 29 flights [as of 2023]. The first ones were most difficult, but each flight you have to make sure you've got everything lined up beforehand. The applications come in and you review them. Then [there is] all the phone calls to all the veterans and guardians. It all has to fall into place and there has to be somebody there to check and double-check that we've got this done," Frank Magsamen said, summarizing the process.

Ask the leaders of Cedar Valley Honor Flight what makes the organization successful and you'll hear very similar responses.

"Everybody had a job. You didn't have to tell them twice or ask them if it was done because it was just done," Janet Liming recalled.

"You know, the committee's really good at what they do. They make sure that what needs to be done gets done," Magsamen said.

"It's the good board members that we have. They just do a good job and get it done," Craig White added.

"I don't do this alone. My team, they're the best!" Linda Bergmann affirmed.

And to a person, the many volunteers who have invested thousands of hours working on behalf of Cedar Valley Honor Flight remain as committed to the mission today as they were in 2011, with Bergmann summing it up best:

"I'll continue this as long as there's interest [from the veterans and community] and money in the bank!"

SIMPLY PUT

Reprinted from the May 25, 2011, edition of The Progress Review.

By Michael Whittlesey

For each of us, there are days that are so memorable they become etched in our minds forever. Your wedding day, the birth of your child, the loss of a loved one, perhaps the events of September 11, 2001, are examples of days that you may recall with remarkable clarity, as if they just happened yesterday. Last week, one such day was added to my list, as I had the good fortune to accompany 91 World War II veterans to Washington, D.C. to visit the World War II Memorial.

As a member of the media, my primary role was to record the events of the day and share the story of the Waterloo Honor Flight with our readers. And what a day it was, one filled with very powerful images.

Two distinct generations, one powerful message of thanks.

Three buses carrying the veterans of the Waterloo Honor Flight and their guardians made several stops during the day, visiting six distinct points of interest. At each of these locations, young teenagers could be seen,

WORKING FOR HUGS - *Patsy DuPre, a member of the Honor Flight Ground Crew and bus tour guide, had a simple explanation for the Washington D.C. area volunteers' commitment to hospitality. "We work for hugs," she said. By the end of the day, she was well compensated.*

spontaneously stepping away from their own tour group to stop and shake hands with a veteran, thanking them for their service. At first, their advances took some of the veterans by surprise. As the day progressed and the young people kept coming at every stop along the tour, the expressions of gratitude became mutual responses from young and old alike. Anyone who has spent time with teenagers knows they are typically focused on the events of the here and now in their own lives. That these young people hailing from several different states would willingly step away from their classmates to thank a stranger some 75 years older was nothing less than remarkable.

Strong hands.

After the students set such a great example on how to thank a veteran, the veterans' guardians decided to do the same at the Iwo Jima Memorial, the final stop of the day. As I waited in the long line to shake

Waterloo, Iowa

On student respect for veterans:

"One particular time I was out there, this whole class [of students], they had so much respect for these veterans. They all came up and thanked them and shook their hands."

~*Janet Schupbach, Honor Flight Organizer*

each veteran's hand, I reminded myself to take it easy when grasping the hands of folks who were probably tired after a long day in the nation's capital. Well, someone forgot to tell these veterans they were supposed to be tired. Handshake after handshake was firm and strong, like the grip of a proud American. As well they should be.

As we pause on Memorial Day to remember those who made the ultimate sacrifice to preserve our freedom, we see the Honor Flight program as a special way to thank and remember those who went to war for our nation over a half century ago. As we thank them, let us also remember the men and women who have worked so hard to make the Waterloo Honor Flights a reality. For it's the ability of a diverse group of individuals working together for a common cause that makes our nation truly great. And to all those who helped make the trips to Washington, D.C. a day our Waterloo area veterans will never forget, we say, "Thank you for YOUR service."

Cedar Valley Honor Flight Story

15

FUND-RAISING

In 2011, the challenge of raising $100,000 to fund one Honor Flight seemed daunting. There can be no denying that the check from Burk and Julie Miehe that year to pay for an entire flight served as an impetus for the Waterloo community to respond accordingly and honor its veterans. 2011 saw Cedar Valley Honor Flight actually sponsor three flights to Washington, D.C. How did the other flights get funded?

With excitement building to send Cedar Valley area World War II veterans on a trip of a lifetime, members of the community opened their hearts and their checkbooks. Soon, donations of $50 and $100 were rolling in. Additional fund-raising events, such as spaghetti suppers, pancake breakfasts and other events sponsored by community organizations helped spread the word and fund Cedar Valley Honor Flight's mission, making it possible for some 300 veterans to see their memorials by the end of 2011.

As the organization brainstormed ideas for a major fund-raiser, the concept of something like a USO Show emerged as a natural fit, as the United Service Organizations have a long and proud history of providing entertainment overseas for America's troops. To explore the possibility further, Frank Magsamen made a call to Barry Remington, an Army veteran who served in Vietnam and has served in multiple leadership positions with AMVETS Post 49 in Cedar Falls.

"I got a call from Frank because our

NOTHING RUNS LIKE A DEERE - *John Deere's strong support for the Waterloo community was evident in Washington, D.C. on May 6, 2014, as the company sponsored the entire cost of a Cedar Valley Honor Flight, including the hats worn by veterans that day.*

AMVETS Post had just put on a variety show and they were searching for people who had done something like that before," Remington recalled.

From that humble beginning, Cedar Valley Honor Flight enlisted the talents of Bill Quibell and his wife Juanita, who assembled a cast of local talent to perform a variety of musical numbers and skits. Packaged with a catered meal, along with a 50-50 raffle and live and silent auctions that featured goods and services donated by area businesses, the annual Variety Show is well-attended and

by far the organization's biggest fund-raiser of the year.

"We've had really good support," said Ed McFarland, noting that the response to letters sent out by his wife's team resulted in several large donations from the community in 2022.

In May 2014, a second Honor Flight was completely funded by another major business entity in the Cedar Valley, John Deere.

And with Cedar Valley Honor Flight's expansion into additional Eastern Iowa counties in recent years, support for veterans remains very strong in the state of Iowa.

Thank You for Your Service

Waterloo, Iowa

On community support for Honor Flights:

"When we contact businesses for donations, everybody is willing to donate to the Honor Flight. I've never had anybody say they wouldn't donate something for the cause. All the support we've received from the community has been great."

~Barb O'Rourke, Honor Flight Organizer

COMMUNITY DONATIONS - *Over the course of thirteen years, a number of check passing photos have been taken for the benefit of Cedar Valley Honor Flight. This one took place on August 13, 2019, as Kendall Lewis presented a check for $6,800 to Ed McFarland, Craig White and Frank Magsamen, while thanking his fellow members of the Midwest Grease Kings Car Club for their generosity and support of Cedar Valley Honor Flight during their annual car show that year.*

VARIETY SHOW - *A large part of Cedar Valley Honor Flight's ability to raise more than $3 million over a 13 year period of time can be attributed to its annual Variety Show, which features entertainment provided by local artists and celebrities. Above, show creator Bill Quibell (left) performs a number with retired Major General and former Attorney General of Iowa, Evan "Curly" Hultman.*

Pre-Flight Meeting

Once veterans and their guardians have been identified for an upcoming Cedar Valley Honor Flight, preparation for an orientation meeting begins in earnest. The meeting is designed to provide everything veterans and guardians need to know about the upcoming trip and comes with several perks. In addition to a meal catered by Hy-Vee, shirts and hats for the upcoming trip are distributed to all the participants, who are also treated to a presentation of the "Table of Honor," which pays tribute to American prisoners of war and those missing in action.

The "meat" of the pre-flight meeting, though, focuses on the important details that will ensure everyone stays safe while having a good experience. As the leader of the group, Linda Bergmann's message to her travelling companions tries to convey important reminders that must be followed with a little humor.

"I try to keep it light-hearted. When I first get up there I'll say, 'How many of you have I talked to on the phone? How many of your wives have I had to talk to in order to get you to do what I want you to do?' I just tell them we're gonna have a great time. All you have to remember is just mind me. Do what I tell you and we'll be just fine. You know, by then they know when they have to be there, what they can and can't bring, and stuff like that. [They need to know] what to expect at the airport because we have to load 165 people, and that's not easy. Stay together. Don't stay too long [at a venue] because we have to keep on schedule," she said.

CEDAR VALLEY HONOR FLIGHT - *Above: The "voice" of Cedar Valley Honor Flight, Craig White. Below: Cedar Valley Honor Flight co-founder Frank Magsamen at the podium during a pre-flight meeting.*

PRE-FLIGHT MEETINGS - *Thanks to the generosity of the Moose Lodge (left) and UAW Local 838, Cedar Valley Honor Flight has enjoyed excellent facilities to conduct pre-flight meetings, where often the ROTC from local schools (right) will conduct the Presentation of Colors as those present recite the Pledge of Allegiance.*

TABLE OF HONOR - *David Grimm and Randy Miller (right) offer a toast to the prisoners of war and missing in action as part of the Table of Honor presentation at a Cedar Valley Honor Flight pre-flight meeting.*

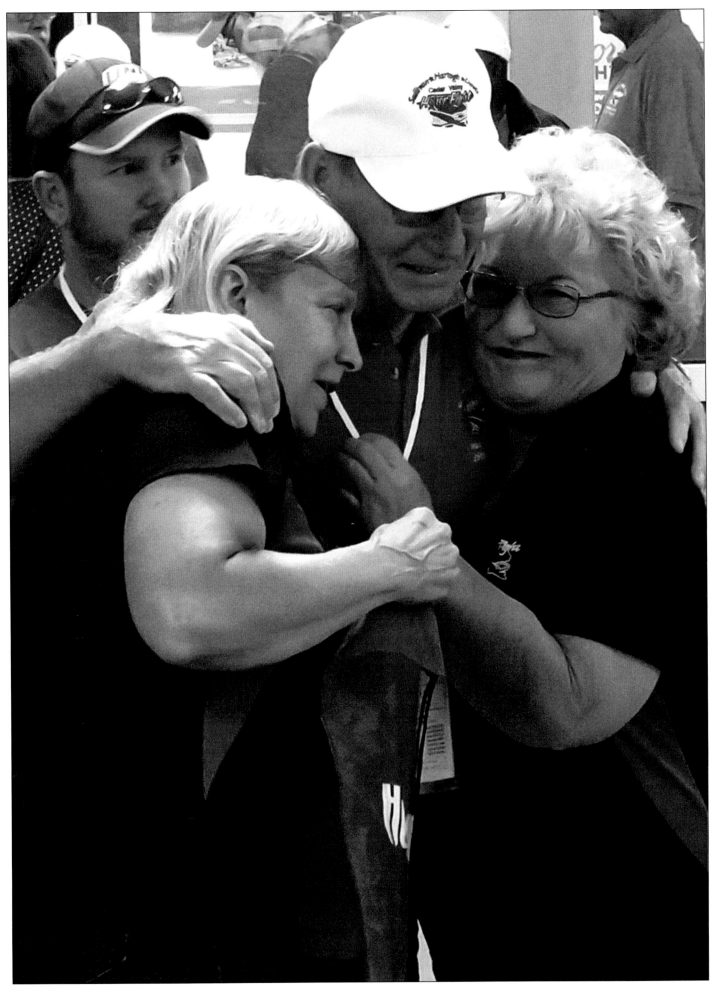

Welcome to Washington, D.C.

Cedar Valley Honor Flights have reached their final destination of Washington, D.C. by way of the three major airports serving the nation's capital. Early flights arrived at Dulles International Airport located in Dulles, Virginia. The organization has also made arrivals at Baltimore-Washington International Thurgood Marshall Airport and Ronald Reagan Washington National Airport.

Many of the Honor Flights originating from Waterloo, Iowa have been greeted with a special water canon salute performed by area Washington, D.C. fire department personnel, who use plumes of water to acknowledge the veterans from both sides of the airplane as it taxis to its gate.

At each of the arrival locations, Cedar Valley veterans have been greeted by a number of dignitaries, military, police and fire department service personnel, as well as local volunteers. Regardless the arrival location, one common sight is the presence of volunteers adorned in brightly colored t-shirts. These Honor Flight Ground Crew members not only greet each incoming flight, they assist veterans and streamline their movement through the terminal to the tour buses that await them. The inscription of a Will Rogers quote on the back of their shirts sums up the spirit of gratitude these volunteers share: "We can't all be heroes - some of us get to stand on the curb and clap as they go by."

Welcome to Washington, D.C.

Welcome to Washington, D.C.

"Oh yay! Oh yay! Oh yay! Welcome our veterans from Waterloo, Iowa!"

WELCOME - *Major General Leslie A. Purser greeted veteran Lyle Dean and Murphy, the first service dog to make a Cedar Valley Honor Flight, at Baltimore-Washington International Airport on May 9, 2017.*

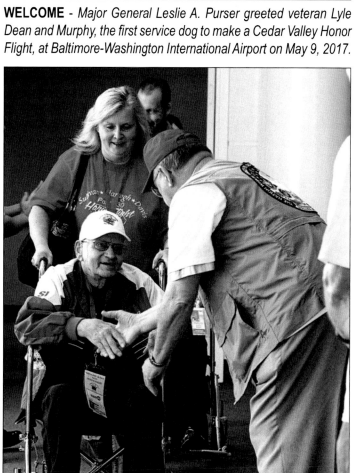

Welcome to Washington, D.C.

Thank You for Your Service

Waterloo, Iowa

On support for Honor Flights in Washington, D.C.:

"When you get out there, there's fire departments shedding arcs of water for the plane to go under. You're greeted by military [personnel] who come onto the plane to talk to the veterans. When you get into the airport, there's volunteers there that help with getting the buses loaded. It's just so huge, the people that are there to make a successful Honor Flight."

~Frank Magsamen, Honor Flight Organizer

Welcome to Washington, D.C.

World War II Memorial

World War II Memorial

"THE GREATEST GENERATION"

Upon entering the World War II Memorial, one is immediately struck by how much there is to see and take in. Dedicated on May 29, 2004, the memorial designed by Friedrich St. Florian is located midway between the Washington Monument and Lincoln Memorial.

At the center of the 7.4 acre site is the Plaza and Rainbow Pool, featuring majestic and elegant plumes of water from two-tiered fountains.

On the north and south ends around the plaza are two semicircular colonnades, each consisting of 28 rectangular pillars 17 feet high, joined by a granite and bronze open balustrade. The 56 pillars represent the 48 states and seven territories that existed during World War II, in addition to the District of Columbia.

At the center of each colonnade is a 43 foot high, four-sided granite arch representing victory and valor, one each for the Atlantic and Pacific theatres. On the west side of the plaza facing east toward the Lincoln Memorial, there are waterfalls on each side of the Freedom Wall, with 4,048 gold stars that symbolize the more than 400,000 American lives lost during World War II.

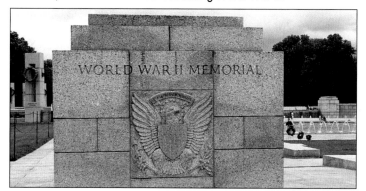

You never know who you're going to meet...

Be it a government official, friend or family member, the World War II Memorial has been a popular place to greet and visit with Cedar Valley Honor Flight veterans.

U.S. Senator Bob Dole

U.S. Representative Rod Blum and U.S. Senator Joni Ernst

"General Dwight D. Eisenhower"

U.S. Representative Bruce Braley

U.S. Representative Ashley Hinson

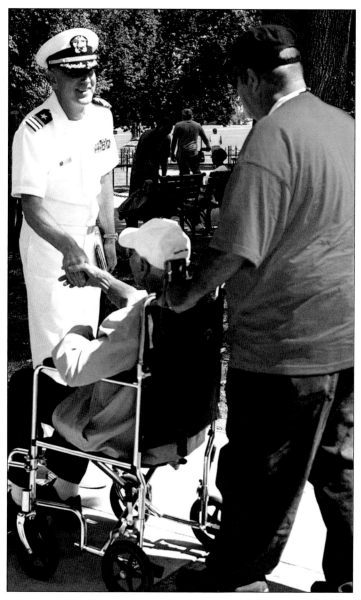

GENERAL DAVID COLE

Waterloo, Iowa native and a member of the West High Class of 1959, David Cole applied to the United States Military Academy at West Point at the behest of his high school principal. The first from his family to serve in the military, there was much to learn at West Point. At the completion of his studies, however, one important commitment had to be honored before his first assignment in the army could begin.

"In three hours after I graduated, my wife and I were married in the West Point chapel. And we've been married ever since," he said.

Cole then went on to a distinguished military career in the United States Army, serving multiple tours in Vietnam. The first came as a First Lieutenant, serving as an advisor to the Vietnamese in the Mekong Delta. He later returned to command an artillery battery, where, despite the close proximity of the enemy, he never lost a single soldier.

Cole eventually was promoted to the rank of Brigadier General before his military career ended. His leadership skills were then put to good use in the private sector, working stints at both Sprint and AOL.

> **" If you don't care for those you are leading, you'll never be a leader. "**
> ~GENERAL DAVID COLE

Retired and living in the Washington, D.C. area, General Cole's close personal friendship with Frank Magsamen, cultivated over many years, has produced a special connection with Cedar Valley Honor Flight. Responding to Magsamen's request in 2011 to meet and greet the first Cedar Valley Honor Flight from their hometown of Waterloo, General Cole and his wife, Connie, were happy to do so. And since that time, every Cedar Valley Honor Flight has had the pleasure of meeting David Cole at the World War II Memorial, attired in full dress uniform and accompanied by his wife of 60 years, where both take the time to pose for photos and visit with his fellow veterans.

In 2016, when Vietnam veterans were first invited to participate in Cedar Valley Honor Flights, the meet and greet opportunities took on an even deeper meaning for General Cole.

"I think what has really changed for me is that I can look into the eyes of my fellow Vietnam veterans. And you see, you see a deep respect and love for one another.

"A lot of them are so happy that somebody from Waterloo who has entered the military and made [the rank of] general is there to greet them, welcome them to Washington, D.C. and thank them for their service. I've said that so many times and it's coming from my heart."

While there's no doubt the Coles are proud to give generously of the their time and show their deep respect for Iowa veterans, their role as "hosts" has come with a few special benefits along the way. Thanks to David's sister and her husband, who had a trailer on the Mississippi River, freshly frozen walleye packed in dry ice were delivered to the Coles, courtesy of Linda Bergmann and Cedar Valley Honor Flight. And on a separate flight, another taste from home came in the form of a special delivery of Iowa pork chops.

Reflecting back on his time in the military, Cole recalls the highs and lows associated with moving from place to place, acknowledging both the benefits and hardships all that travel imposed on his family.

"Not one time did I think I was going to make the military a career. It was just one assignment after another. And I was going to do the best I could at that.

It was a challenge every single day."

On transporting the General's pork chops:

"One time, he was talking to his wife about how much they missed Iowa pork chops. So his sister said, 'I'll talk to Linda and see if she'll bring you some.' I said, 'Are you nuts? I gotta carry pork chops? [laughing]' She said, 'Well, you don't have to.' I said, 'I'll do it for Dave.' And, of course, he sent me a picture when he grilled them. It was worth it. He was so grateful."

~*Linda Bergmann, Honor Flight Organizer*

World War II Memorial

CEDAR VALLEY VETS WELCOMED - *General David Cole and his wife, Connie (above, far left), have greeted veterans at the World War II Memorial in Washington, D.C. on each of the Cedar Valley Honor Flights from Waterloo, Iowa.*

THE PRICE OF FREEDOM

Stationed in front of the wall of gold stars at the World War II Memorial, a plaque is engraved with the following words:

"Freedom Wall holds 4,048 gold stars. Each gold star represents 100 American service personnel who died or remain missing in the war. The 405,399 American dead or missing from World War II are second only to the loss of 620,000 Americans during our Civil War."

During World War II, when families sent a loved one off to fight, it was customary to display a flag in a window containing a blue star bordered in red. Upon notification of that family member's death, the star was replaced with a gold one, revealing the family's sacrifice.

World War II Memorial

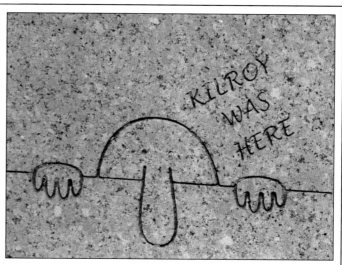

KILROY WAS HERE - A popular piece of World War II graffiti, Kilroy was a cartoon figure drawn by American troops, first in the Atlantic Theater then, later in the Pacific Theater. Its origins are believed to be traced back to a British cartoon and an American shipyard inspector. As Kilroy's popularity grew, his likeness was found nearly everywhere- on ship holds, bridges, bathrooms, even painted on the bombs and missiles of United States aircraft. Two inscriptions of Kilroy can be found at the World War II Memorial, one each in the corners of the Atlantic and Pacific sides of the memorial.

QUOTATIONS AND INSCRIPTIONS

"HERE IN THE PRESENCE OF WASHINGTON AND LINCOLN, ONE THE EIGHTEENTH CENTURY FATHER AND THE OTHER THE NINETEENTH CENTURY PRESERVER OF OUR NATION, WE HONOR THOSE TWENTIETH CENTURY AMERICANS WHO TOOK UP THE STRUGGLE DURING THE SECOND WORLD WAR AND MADE THE SACRIFICES TO PERPETUATE THE GIFT OUR FOREFATHERS ENTRUSTED TO US: A NATION CONCEIVED IN LIBERTY AND JUSTICE."

~World War II Memorial Announcement Stone

Throughout the World War II Memorial, numerous quotations can be found from major military and political figures from the World War II era, including General Dwight D. Eisenhower, Presidents Franklin D. Roosevelt and Harry S. Truman, Admiral Chester W. Nimitz, Generals George C. Marshall and Douglas MacArthur and Colonel Oveta Culp Hobby.

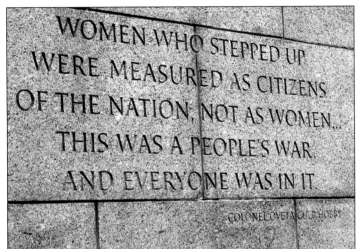

THE WAR'S END

TODAY THE GUNS ARE SILENT. A GREAT TRAGEDY
HAS ENDED. A GREAT VICTORY HAS BEEN WON. THE SKIES
NO LONGER RAIN DEATH—THE SEAS BEAR ONLY COMMERCE—
MEN EVERYWHERE WALK UPRIGHT IN THE SUNLIGHT.
THE ENTIRE WORLD IS QUIETLY AT PEACE.

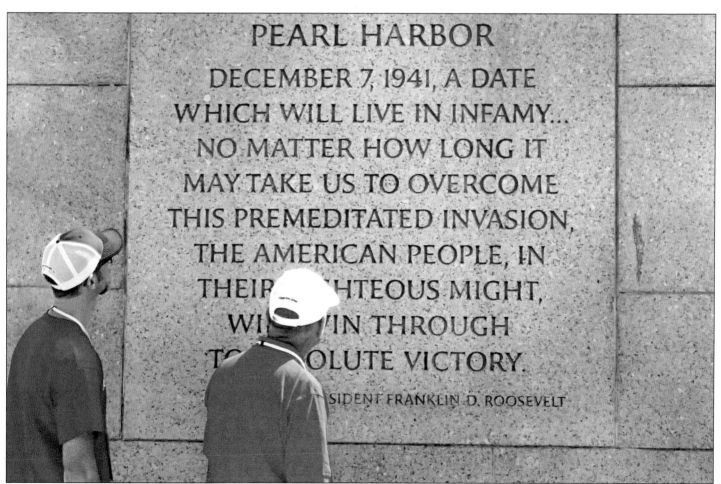

PEARL HARBOR

DECEMBER 7, 1941, A DATE
WHICH WILL LIVE IN INFAMY...
NO MATTER HOW LONG IT
MAY TAKE US TO OVERCOME
THIS PREMEDITATED INVASION,
THE AMERICAN PEOPLE, IN
THEIR RIGHTEOUS MIGHT,
WILL WIN THROUGH
TO ABSOLUTE VICTORY.

—PRESIDENT FRANKLIN D. ROOSEVELT

ATLANTIC

ATLANTIC

TEXAS

KANS

WE ARE DETERMINED
THAT BEFORE THE SUN SETS ON THIS
TERRIBLE STRUGGLE OUR FLAG WILL BE RECOGNIZED
THROUGHOUT THE WORLD AS A SYMBOL OF FREEDOM
ON THE ONE HAND AND OF OVERWHELMING
FORCE ON THE OTHER.

D-DAY JUNE 6, 1944

NORTH AFRICA

BATTLE OF THE ATLANTIC · MURMANSK RUN · TUNISIA · SICILY SALERNO

World War II Memorial

World War II Memorial

Thank You for Your Service

Waterloo, Iowa

On serving World War II veterans, "The Greatest Generation":

"Those guys were so humble, so moved and so thankful. Sometimes you would walk down the aisle and you would see some of them just sitting there with tears running down their face. It was an emotional time for them."

~Teresa Schmitz, Honor Flight Organizer

World War II Memorial

Thank You for Your Service

Waterloo, Iowa

On serving as an Honor Flight guardian:

"We went around and I took pictures everywhere. And I made a Shutterfly book for him. He was really touched by that and I just really appreciated learning from him. On the flight home [during Mail Call] he was reading his his mail and he was very emotional. He handed me this letter from one of his best friends that said how proud his parents would be of him for his service. There's just so much emotion [for these veterans] from what they did to what they continue to do. They're like a family."

~Sue Gress, Honor Flight Organizer

A Tour of Washington, D.C.

FLAGS ACROSS ROSSLYN - Each year, building owners in the unincorporated area of Rosslyn in Arlington, Virginia, fly large American flags on their buildings to commemorate the 9/11 terrorist attacks on the Pentagon and World Trade Center. This image was captured during a September 10, 2019 Cedar Valley Honor Flight.

WASHINGTON, D.C.

Washington, D.C., bordered on the east and west by the Anacostia and Potomac rivers, respectively, is a federal district created in 1790. The city was designed by Pierre Charles L'Enfant, an American-French military engineer. D.C. stands for District of Columbia, a name chosen to honor the explorer Christopher Columbus.

THE WHITE HOUSE

With so many sights to see in a limited amount of time, Honor Flight organizers must be ready to adapt to any unforeseen circumstances that may occur and threaten the scheduled itinerary. A quick driving tour of the nation's capital is one way to build flex time into the day. On those occasions when the airplane and bus schedules have gone as planned, Cedar Valley Honor Flight veterans have been treated to some bonus views of Washington, D.C.. For the photographers along for the ride, a window seat and a little luck, as landmarks zip by with traffic all around, can result in some interesting shots. On two occasions, photographers captured these images of the White House, home to every United States president except George Washington, who died before it was built.

U.S. CAPITOL

All roads in Washington, D.C. lead to the United States Capitol building, the dividing center for all the city's quadrants. Construction of the U.S. Capitol, which began in 1793, was completed in 1800. Over the years, a number of extensions have been added, the last being completed in 1962.

The Capitol building features 540 rooms and 658 windows. A total of 108 windows are part of the Capitol dome, which is made primarily of cast iron and weighs just under nine million pounds. Sitting atop the dome is the 19.5 foot tall Statue of Freedom, which depicts a female figure wearing a military helmet, holding a sheathed sword in her right hand and a laurel wreath and shield in her left.

A restoration of the Capitol building began in 2014 and was completed in November 2016. Photos from Cedar Valley Honor Flights during those years show the various stages of the repairs being made.

THOMAS JEFFERSON MEMORIAL

As illustrated by the two early Honor Flight photos above, pictures of the Jefferson Memorial can be found from a variety of angles during a day spent in Washington, D.C.. The top left photo, taken in September 2014, is unique in that the tour bus was close enough to offer a view of Jefferson himself, the only time an image of this imposing 18 foot high statue standing within the colonnade was captured on a Cedar Valley Honor Flight.

In 2019, the National Park Service initiated a restoration project to restore the roofs, repair the stone and clean the marble of the Thomas Jefferson Memorial. Evidence of the work in progress could be seen during a September 2019 Honor Flight (middle right photo). Special lasers were used to remove a layer of black biofilm, a combination of algae, fungi and bacteria growing on the Memorial's roof. When Cedar Valley Honor Flight returned in September 2022, the project's completion revealed a significant transformation (lower right photo).

Thomas Jefferson was the nation's third president, remembered as the primary author of the Declaration of Independence and for nearly doubling the size of the United States with the Louisiana Purchase in 1803.

WASHINGTON MONUMENT

Standing over 555 feet high, it is fitting that the monument honoring our nation's first president can be seen from virtually any vantage point in Washington, D.C.. As Cedar Valley Honor Flight veterans enjoy each stop along the day-long tour of the nation's capital, it is not uncommon to find images of the Washington Monument in the background as part of their visits to the World War II Memorial, Vietnam Memorial, United States Air Force Memorial and other locations. On August 23, 2011, a 5.8 magnitude earthquake occurred 84 miles southwest of Washington, D.C., damaging the Washington Monument. After 32 months of restoration, the world's tallest free-standing stone structure and tallest obelisk was reopened to the public on May 12, 2014.

June 2013

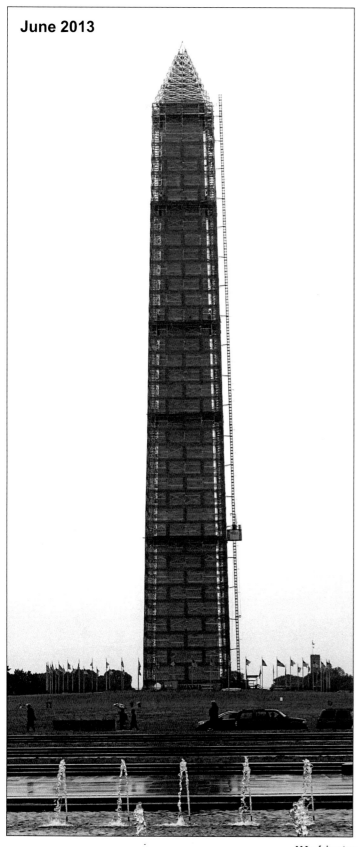

June 2016

LOCKKEEPER'S HOUSE - Built in 1837, the Lockkeeper's House is the oldest building in Washington, D.C.. The structure dates back to a time when the south end of 17th Street, where the building currently sits, was part of the Washington City Canal used for the transportation of heavy goods for developing railroads. At that time, the lockkeeper was needed to collect tolls and for record keeping. The building was abandoned in 1855 with the downfall of the canal. In 1903, with the building in a state of disrepair, it was renovated to serve as the headquarters for the United States Park Police and outfitted with a holding cell. By 1940, the building's first floor was used primarily for storage and restrooms before eventually sitting in a boarded up state for forty years. As the land where the canal once flowed was reclaimed and traffic increased in the area, the National Park Service restored the building's exterior to its 1800s appearance, where it now serves as a National Park Service education center.

THE PENTAGON - The world's second largest office building, the Pentagon (above), was constructed during World War II and serves as the headquarters for the Department of Defense. With 6.5 million square feet of floor space, the Pentagon features five floors above ground, two basement levels and five rings of corridors per floor for a total of 17.5 miles of corridors. On September 11, 2001, five al-Qaeda terrorists flew American Airlines Flight 77 into the western side of the building, killing a total of 189 people, 64 on the airplane and 125 on the ground. As part of the repairs, a small indoor memorial and chapel were added at the point of impact. An outdoor memorial for the the Pentagon victims of 9/11 was dedicated on September 11, 2008.

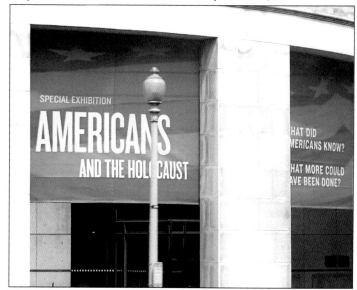

THE SECOND DIVISION

TOULON-
TROYON
BOIS
DE
BELLEAU
VAUX
SOISSONS.

MARBAC
ST. MIHI
BLANC MC
MEUSE
ARGONN
THE RH

TO OUR DEAD

Washington, D.C. Tour

Korean War Memorial

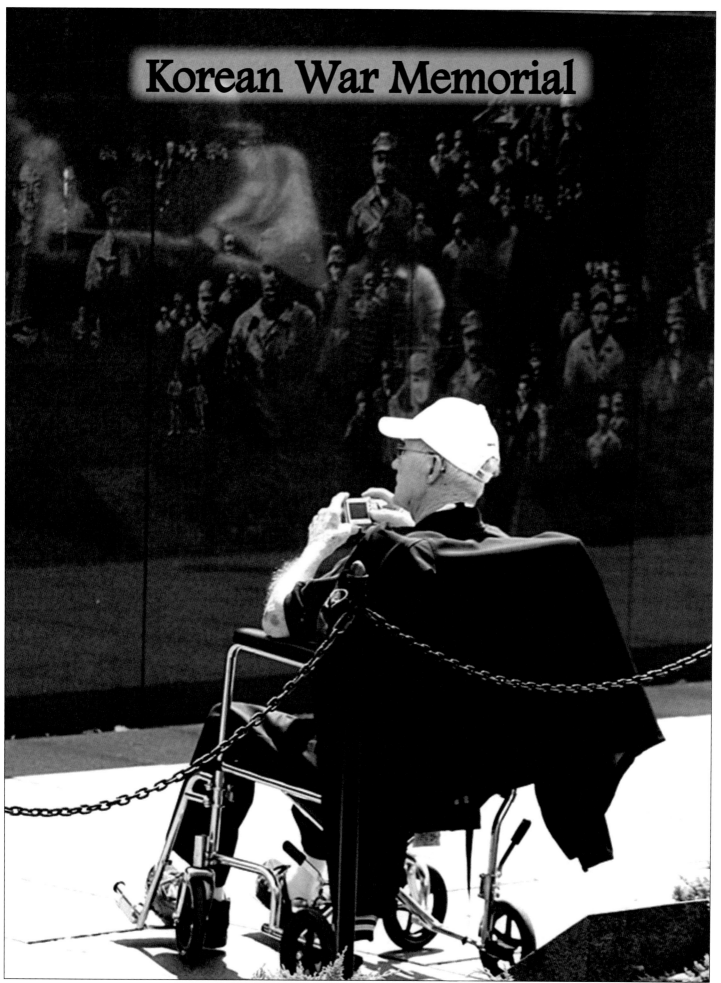

Field of Service

The soldiers that appear in the Korean War Memorial are 19 stainless steel statues sculpted by Frank Gaylord of Barre, Vermont and cast by Tallix Foundries of Beacon, New York. They are approximately seven feet tall, weigh close to 1,000 pounds each and represent an ethnic cross section of America. This composition is symbolically important because the Korean War was the first conflict since the American Revolution that U.S. military troops were not segregated by race.

The soldiers represent an advance party on patrol, depicting each of the four major branches of service: 14 Army, three Marine, one Navy and one Air Force, for a total of 19 service members. The statues stand among patches of juniper bushes and polished granite strips, which give a semblance of order and symbolizes the rice paddies of Korea. The troops wear ponchos covering their weapons and equipment, an indication of the harsh weather conditions that existed during the conflict.

It should be noted that wherever visitors are on the memorial grounds, the eyes of at least one soldier will be upon them.

Korean War Memorial

THE MURAL WALL

Designed by Louis Nelson of New York, New York and fabricated by Cold Spring Granite Company of Cold Spring, Minnesota, the mural wall depicts images of the Korean War on 41 panels that extend 164 feet in length. Working closely together, the muralist, sculptor and architect created a wall featuring two-dimensional art designed to complement the adjacent three-dimensional statues. To accomplish this goal, over 2,400 photographs of the Korean War were obtained from the National Archives, then enhanced by computer to create a uniform lighting effect and scale them to the desired size.

Images on the mural illustrate the forces that supported the foot soldiers represented by the memorial's 19 stainless steel statues. They include service personnel and equipment from the Army, Navy, Marine Corps, Air Force and Coast Guard. While photographs were used as a basis for the illustrations etched into the black granite wall, special care was taken to ensure the anonymity of the soldiers depicted upon it.

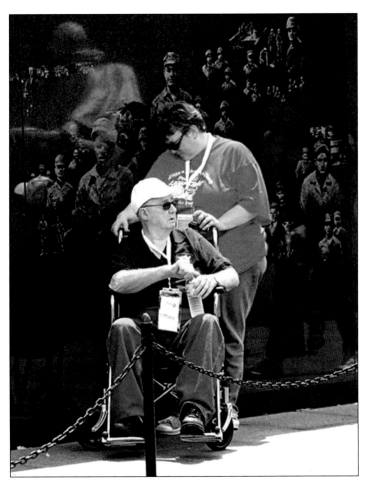

The reflective quality of the wall itself adds to the symbolism of the memorial while gazing at it, creating an image that totals 38 statues, a deliberate nod to the 38th parallel where the war took place and the 38 months of its duration.

The Korean War Memorial, designed by Cooper-Lecky Architects, sits on 2.2 acres of ground located near the Lincoln Memorial on the National Mall. The memorial honors the 5.8 million Americans who served in the United States Armed Forces during the three year period of the conflict, with 36,634 killed, listed as missing in action, lost or buried at sea.

Korean War Memorial

WALL OF REMEMBRANCE

As part of a $22 million renovation of the Korean War Memorial undertaken in 2021, the Wall of Remembrance was constructed. The wall contains the names of the more than 36,000 American service personnel and over 7,100 Koreans who lost their lives during the Korean War. Spanning 100 panels, the Wall of Remembrance is organized by branch of service and rank. It serves as a stark reminder of how the burden of war was felt most severely by the lowest ranks of the military, as 44 of the 84 panels devoted to the U.S. Army contain the names of privates and privates first class.

The Korean War Memorial renovation, completed and opened to the public on July 27, 2022, included a refinishing of the 19 stainless steel statues of soldiers. In addition to other cosmetic improvements at the memorial, the juniper trees in the Field of Service and linden trees around the Pool of Remembrance were also replaced.

OUR NATION HONORS
HER SONS AND DAUGHTERS
WHO ANSWERED THE CALL
TO DEFEND A COUNTRY
THEY NEVER KNEW
AND A PEOPLE
THEY NEVER MET

1950 ▪ KOREA ▪ 1953

UNITED STATES AIR FORCE

AIRMAN

ORVILLE E ASHBAKER
EUGENE B BRAUNSDORF
CHAUNCEY E COLEMAN
ELEODORO R FERNANDEZ
JOHN A MATHEWS
WALLACE A MEBANE
DUWAYNE C MORTIMER
JAMES J RIVERS
CHARLES C SANDS
HOWARD W TILLOTSON

AIRMAN
THIRD CLASS

JOSEPH C JAMIESON
GERALD E JOHNSON
GEORGE D JONES JR
GERALD JONES
JIMMIE L KAHANEK
LEWELLYN K KALEPA
EDWARD KAZMIERCZAK
JOHN KOTORA JR
DUANE W LARSON
EDWARD R LOGSTON
JOHN W MASLIN
RICHARD MASON
JAMES MCCORMICK
BERNARD F MCEVOY
RONALD G MCGRATH
JOHN G MCMANN
DAVID E MILES
ARLEN J MORGAN

FREEDOM IS NOT FREE

Korean War Memorial

Lincoln Memorial

The Lincoln Memorial sits in a place of honor on the west end of the National Mall, extending a line from the U.S. Capitol and the Washington Monument. Two years after Lincoln's assassination in 1865, Congress passed the first of several bills to create a memorial dedicated to him. It wasn't until 1911, however, when Congress created a new Lincoln Memorial Commission, that plans began to make progress. At the time, the proposed location for the memorial was controversial, as work on reclaiming the west end of the National Mall from the Potomac River was ongoing and opponents viewed the area as a swamp.

The Lincoln Memorial Commission eventually selected architect Henry Bacon to design the memorial and Daniel Chester French to sculpt a statue of President Lincoln. Eight years after the ground-breaking ceremony in 1914, Chief Justice of the United States (and former president) William Howard Taft dedicated the memorial on May 30, 1922, with Lincoln's only surviving son, Robert Todd Lincoln, in attendance.

Bacon, who felt that the man who defended democracy should have a memorial that paid tribute to the birthplace of it, modeled his design after the Parthenon in Athens, Greece. The massive memorial measures 190 feet long, 120 feet wide, 99 feet tall and was constructed with Colorado Yule marble. It features 36 doric columns, symbolic of the number of states at the time of Lincoln's death. Each of the columns tilt slightly inward to prevent the structure from appearing top-heavy. Above the columns engraved on the frieze are the names of the 36 states and the dates they entered the union.

Lincoln's statue was originally designed to be ten feet tall but it quickly became apparent that such a size would be way too small to fill the chamber space. Enlarged to stand 19 feet tall and 19 feet wide, the statue consists of Georgia white marble, weighs 175 tons and had to be shipped to Washington, D.C. in 28 separate pieces. It took Daniel Chester French four years to complete the work, who wanted the finished product to reflect both Lincoln's strength and compassionate nature. To accomplish this, he positioned one of Lincoln's hands with a clenched fist to illustrate his strength and determination, with the other hand slightly open and more relaxed to portray his compassionate, warm nature.

There are 87 steps leading up to the chamber from the reflecting pool, symbolic of the opening line of the Gettysburg Address and Lincoln's reference to "Four score and seven years ago..."

The Lincoln Memorial has long been a symbol of freedom and dignity for all peoples, serving as the site for Reverend Martin Luther King, Jr.'s "I Have a Dream" speech in 1963 in front of 200,000 people during the March on Washington.

FELLOW COUNTRYMEN : AT THIS SECOND APPEARING TO TAKE THE OATH OF THE PRESIDENTIAL OFFICE THERE IS LESS OCCASION FOR AN EXTENDED ADDRESS THAN THERE WAS AT THE FIRST · THEN A STATEMENT SOMEWHAT IN DETAIL OF A COURSE TO BE PURSUED SEEMED FITTING AND PROPER · NOW AT THE EXPIRATION OF FOUR YEARS DURING WHICH PUBLIC DECLARATIONS HAVE BEEN CONSTANTLY CALLED FORTH ON EVERY POINT AND PHASE OF THE GREAT CONTEST WHICH STILL ABSORBS THE ATTENTION AND ENGROSSES THE ENERGIES OF THE NATION LITTLE THAT IS NEW COULD BE PRESENTED · THE PROGRESS OF OUR ARMS UPON WHICH ALL ELSE CHIEFLY DEPENDS IS AS WELL KNOWN TO THE PUBLIC AS TO MYSELF AND IT IS I TRUST REASONABLY SATISFACTORY AND ENCOURAGING TO ALL · WITH HIGH HOPE FOR THE FUTURE NO PREDICTION IN REGARD TO IT IS VENTURED · ON THE OCCASION CORRESPONDING TO THIS FOUR YEARS AGO ALL THOUGHTS WERE ANXIOUSLY DIRECTED TO AN IMPENDING CIVIL WAR · ALL DREADED IT—ALL SOUGHT TO AVERT IT · WHILE THE INAUGURAL ADDRESS WAS BEING DELIVERED FROM THIS PLACE DEVOTED ALTOGETHER TO SAVING THE UNION WITHOUT WAR INSURGENT AGENTS WERE IN THE CITY SEEKING TO DESTROY IT WITHOUT WAR—SEEKING TO DISSOLVE THE UNION AND DIVIDE EFFECTS BY NEGOTIATION · BOTH PARTIES DEPRECATED WAR BUT ONE OF THEM WOULD MAKE WAR RATHER THAN LET THE NATION SURVIVE

AND THE OTHER WOULD ACCEPT WAR RATHER THAN LET IT PERISH · AND THE WAR CAME · ONE EIGHTH OF THE WHOLE POPULATION WERE COLORED SLAVES NOT DISTRIBUTED GENERALLY OVER THE UNION BUT LOCALIZED IN THE SOUTHERN PART OF IT · THESE SLAVES CONSTITUTED A PECULIAR AND POWERFUL INTEREST · ALL KNEW THAT THIS INTEREST WAS SOMEHOW THE CAUSE OF THE WAR · TO STRENGTHEN PERPETUATE AND EXTEND THIS INTEREST WAS THE OBJECT FOR WHICH THE INSURGENTS WOULD REND THE UNION EVEN BY WAR WHILE THE GOVERNMENT CLAIMED NO RIGHT TO DO MORE THAN TO RESTRICT THE TERRITORIAL ENLARGEMENT OF IT · NEITHER PARTY EXPECTED FOR THE WAR THE MAGNITUDE OR THE DURATION WHICH IT HAS ALREADY ATTAINED · NEITHER ANTICIPATED THAT THE CAUSE OF THE CONFLICT MIGHT CEASE WITH OR EVEN BEFORE THE CONFLICT ITSELF SHOULD CEASE · EACH LOOKED FOR AN EASIER TRIUMPH AND A RESULT LESS FUNDAMENTAL AND ASTOUNDING · BOTH READ THE SAME BIBLE AND PRAY TO THE SAME GOD AND EACH INVOKES HIS AID AGAINST THE OTHER · IT MAY SEEM STRANGE THAT ANY MEN SHOULD DARE TO ASK A JUST GOD'S ASSISTANCE IN WRINGING THEIR BREAD FROM THE SWEAT OF OTHER MEN'S FACES BUT LET US JUDGE NOT THAT WE BE NOT JUDGED · THE PRAYERS OF BOTH COULD NOT BE ANSWERED—THAT OF NEITHER HAS BEEN ANSWERED FULLY · THE ALMIGHTY HAS HIS OWN PURPOSES · "WOE UNTO THE WORLD BECAUSE OF OFFENSES FOR IT MUST NEEDS BE THAT OFFENSES COME BUT WOE TO THAT MAN BY WHOM THE OFFENSE COMETH."

IF WE SHALL SUPPOSE THAT AMERICAN SLAVERY IS ONE OF THOSE OFFENSES WHICH IN THE PROVIDENCE OF GOD MUST NEEDS COME BUT WHICH HAVING CONTINUED THROUGH HIS APPOINTED TIME HE NOW WILLS TO REMOVE AND THAT HE GIVES TO BOTH NORTH AND SOUTH THIS TERRIBLE WAR AS THE WOE DUE TO THOSE BY WHOM THE OFFENSE CAME SHALL WE DISCERN THEREIN ANY DEPARTURE FROM THOSE DIVINE ATTRIBUTES WHICH THE BELIEVERS IN A LIVING GOD ALWAYS ASCRIBE TO HIM · FONDLY DO WE HOPE—FERVENTLY DO WE PRAY—THAT THIS MIGHTY SCOURGE OF WAR MAY SPEEDILY PASS AWAY · YET IF GOD WILLS THAT IT CONTINUE UNTIL ALL THE WEALTH PILED BY THE BONDSMAN'S TWO HUNDRED AND FIFTY YEARS OF UNREQUITED TOIL SHALL BE SUNK AND UNTIL EVERY DROP OF BLOOD DRAWN WITH THE LASH SHALL BE PAID BY ANOTHER DRAWN WITH THE SWORD AS WAS SAID THREE THOUSAND YEARS AGO SO STILL IT MUST BE SAID "THE JUDGMENTS OF THE LORD ARE TRUE AND RIGHTEOUS ALTOGETHER." WITH MALICE TOWARD NONE WITH CHARITY FOR ALL WITH FIRMNESS IN THE RIGHT AS GOD GIVES US TO SEE THE RIGHT LET US STRIVE ON TO FINISH THE WORK WE ARE IN TO BIND UP THE NATION'S WOUNDS TO CARE FOR HIM WHO SHALL HAVE BORNE THE BATTLE AND FOR HIS WIDOW AND HIS ORPHAN TO DO ALL WHICH MAY ACHIEVE AND CHERISH A JUST AND LASTING PEACE AMONG OURSELVES AND WITH ALL NATIONS.

FOUR SCORE AND SEVEN YEARS AGO OUR FATHERS BROUGHT FORTH ON THIS CONTINENT A NEW NATION CONCEIVED IN LIBERTY AND DEDICATED TO THE PROPOSITION THAT ALL MEN ARE CREATED EQUAL ·

NOW WE ARE ENGAGED IN A GREAT CIVIL WAR TESTING WHETHER THAT NATION OR ANY NATION SO CONCEIVED AND SO DEDICATED CAN LONG ENDURE · WE ARE MET ON A GREAT BATTLEFIELD OF THAT WAR · WE HAVE COME TO DEDICATE A PORTION OF THAT FIELD AS A FINAL RESTING PLACE FOR THOSE WHO HERE GAVE THEIR LIVES THAT THAT NATION MIGHT LIVE · IT IS ALTOGETHER FITTING AND PROPER THAT WE SHOULD DO THIS · BUT IN A LARGER SENSE WE CAN NOT DEDICATE~WE CAN NOT CONSECRATE~WE CAN NOT HALLOW~ THIS GROUND · THE BRAVE MEN LIVING AND DEAD WHO STRUGGLED HERE HAVE CONSECRATED IT FAR ABOVE OUR POOR POWER TO ADD OR DETRACT · THE WORLD WILL LITTLE NOTE NOR LONG REMEMBER WHAT WE SAY HERE BUT IT CAN NEVER FORGET WHAT THEY DID HERE · IT IS FOR US THE LIVING RATHER TO BE DEDICATED HERE TO THE UNFINISHED WORK WHICH THEY WHO FOUGHT HERE HAVE THUS FAR SO NOBLY ADVANCED · IT IS RATHER FOR US TO BE HERE DEDICATED TO THE GREAT TASK REMAINING BEFORE US~ THAT FROM THESE HONORED DEAD WE TAKE INCREASED DEVOTION TO THAT CAUSE FOR WHICH THEY GAVE THE LAST FULL MEASURE OF DEVOTION ~ THAT WE HERE HIGHLY RESOLVE THAT THESE DEAD SHALL NOT HAVE DIED IN VAIN ~ THAT THIS NATION UNDER GOD SHALL HAVE A NEW BIRTH OF FREEDOM~ AND THAT GOVERNMENT OF THE PEOPLE BY THE PEOPLE FOR THE PEOPLE SHALL NOT PERISH FROM THE EARTH ·

Lincoln Memorial

MARINE SILENT DRILL PLATOON - *On May 11, 2022, Cedar Valley Honor Flight veterans were treated to a performance by "The Marching Twenty-Four," a unique silent precision exhibition of Marines in front of the Lincoln Memorial.*

IN THIS TEMPLE
AS IN THE HEARTS OF THE PEOPLE
FOR WHOM HE SAVED THE UNION
THE MEMORY OF ABRAHAM LINCOLN
IS ENSHRINED FOREVER

Vietnam War Memorial

"THE WALL"

Maya Ying Lin's design for the Vietnam War Memorial, dedicated November 11, 1982, is filled with symbolism:

• •

Lin used v-shaped walls embedded into the landscape to symbolize a healing wound, much like the war was a source of trauma in America.

• •

Unlike the white marble present in so many Washington, D.C. monuments, Lin chose the color black for the walls because the color is symbolic of earth.

• •

Black granite, when polished, becomes reflective like a mirror. Lin believed it was important for visitors to see themselves as they touched the names of those who died, to remember they were just like them.

• •

Lin listed 58,318 names in chronological order, rather than alphabetical, so that soldiers who fought and died together would always be together on the wall. Rather than start the names on one end of the memorial, she began them in the middle, where the panels are tallest.

• •

From the center of the wall, proceeding east toward the Washington Monument, 29,000 names are presented.

• •

Beginning with those who died in 1954, the wall recedes into the earth at the end on May 25, 1968, the half-way point of American casualties. Moving around to the other end, the names pick up and continue on that same day in 1968, proceeding to the center of the memorial, where the final 18 American casualties appear on the panel adjacent to those who died first. Lin designed the memorial this way so the first and last would always be together.

• •

Lin designed the eastern wall to point to the Washington Monument and the western wall to the Lincoln Memorial, cradling the memorial between two great presidents, giving it an historical place on the National Mall.

• •

The Vietnam War Memorial contains no references to rank, gender or nationality. On this wall, everyone is equal.

Thank You for Your Service

Sullivan ★ Hartogh ★ Davis
Cedar Valley
Honor Flight
Waterloo

Waterloo, Iowa

On "laying it down" at The Wall:

"It changed my life quite a bit. Me and two of my best buddies went out to D.C. and got out to The Wall. It was early evening and it was sprinkling. All three of us didn't say a word, just standing there, thinking about what we'd been through. We didn't serve together but we knew one other well. All of a sudden, one buddy of mine said, 'Do you see what I see?' And I said, 'I'm not sure what you see.' He said, 'Doesn't it look like The Wall is crying?' With the rain, it looked like tears were coming out of The Wall. 'Now that I look at it again,' I said, 'it looks like it does.' We stood there and talked about that for quite awhile and went around and showed each other the names of the guys that we served with that didn't come home. And that's when it really hit home. Then you sit there and you think to yourself, 'Maybe I should be a different person. Maybe I shouldn't be the jackass that I'd been for a long time and I got a different perspective on life. A short period of time after it hit home, I got involved in volunteering and a lot of other stuff. It helped me turn my life around."

~Craig White, Honor Flight Organizer

Vietnam War Memorial

SIMPLY PUT

Reprinted from the June 1, 2016 edition of *The Progress Review*:

By Michael Whittlesey

Last week, more than 90 veterans from eastern and central Iowa were aboard the 15th Honor Flight sponsored by Sullivan-Hartogh-Davis Post 730 in Waterloo. *The Progress Review* has been fortunate to have a photographer along for the ride for 14 of those flights, as part of our commitment to provide each veteran with a commemorative DVD documenting their experience in Washington DC. Last week's trip marked the first opportunity for Waterloo area veterans of the Vietnam War to make an Honor Flight, and more than 60 of the 90+ veterans aboard the flight served their country during that conflict.

Prior to the flight, I wondered if this first trip with Vietnam veterans to Washington would make for a different Honor Flight experience. It most certainly did, and in a way that was far more powerful than I could have imagined.

The challenge of shooting photos and video on the journey from Waterloo to Washington, D.C. and back makes for a very busy day. That's what makes the time spent in the air so enjoyable. The two hour flight provides an excellent opportunity to meet and visit with some of the veterans, always an educational experience when they describe their time in the military.

On this trip, I sat next to a veteran who spoke about serving on an LST (Landing Ship, Tank), a ship designed to support amphibious operations by carrying vehicles, cargo, and landing troops directly onto an unimproved shore. While serving in Vietnam, he described an incredibly harrowing experience, a sneak attack carried out by the enemy that claimed the lives of seventeen of his shipmates.

Researching the incident, I learned that at 3:22 AM on November 1, 1968, two large mines were detonated on the starboard side of the U.S.S. Westchester County (LST-1167). Boiler Technician Gary Wood, from Decorah, Iowa, was one of the lucky crew members who survived the initial attack. In the moments after the blast, his responsibility was to seal a door below deck to help prevent the ship from sinking.

Chest deep in water and oil, Gary knew that sealing the door would more than likely also seal the fate of anyone still alive in that compartment, a thought, he said, he has had to live with since that fateful day.

Forty-eight years later, as he prepared to visit the Vietnam War Memorial for the first time, Gary Wood carried with him a small piece of paper upon which he had written several names.

"These are my guys!" he told me.

A unique feature about the Vietnam War Memorial is that the names inscribed upon the wall are listed chronologically, so that those who served and died together will forever be memorialized together on the black granite. Gary's search for his brothers, the shipmates who lost their lives while serving their country nearly 50 years ago, would take him to panels 39 and 40 of the west wall. Among the names listed there were the following U.S. Navy sailors: Jackie C Carter, Richard C Cartwright, Chester D Dale, Keith William Duffy, Timothy C Dunning, David G Fell, Thomas G Funke, Gerald E B Hamm, Floyd Houghtaling III, Aristotoles D Ibanez, Jerry S Leonard, Joesph A Miller Jr, Rodney W Peters, Cary F Rundle, Reinhard J Schnurrer Jr, Thomas H Smith, Anthony R Torcivia.

Gary would later admit to getting emotional at that moment. Who could blame him? Standing there with a camera in my hand, it didn't feel right to point it in his direction, as this very personal moment played out among the hundreds of people who were milling about. Looking up and down along the 246 feet of polished granite, Gary was not alone in his emotion. Tears were evident as other veterans, family members and friends located the names for whom they searched. Some stood quietly, while others kneeled at the wall, deep in prayer.

The Vietnam War Memorial Wall was constructed in 1982 in an effort to heal the scars, still evident today, that this controversial war left behind. Standing there in the bright sunshine on a beautiful day in the nation's capital, I was reminded why the Honor Flight program is so beneficial for the veterans who make the trip to Washington, D.C.. It's a journey that is perhaps even more important for our Vietnam War veterans, the men and women who did not receive the homecoming they deserved for their service to the nation.

Finally, as I ascended the walkway to return to our tour bus, I couldn't help but think how glad Gary's guys must have been that he stopped by to pay them a visit.

Vietnam War Memorial

Vietnam War Memorial

Vietnam War Memorial

Thank You for Your Service

Sullivan ★ Hartogh ★ Davis
Cedar Valley
Honor Flight
Waterloo

Waterloo, Iowa

On "laying it down":

"When he [a Vietnam veteran] came back, he said, 'That was one of the best things that could have happened to me. I unloaded a lot of stuff there.' And I said, 'Well, that's what it's for.'"

~Barry Remington, Honor Flight Organizer

VIETNAM WOMEN'S MEMORIAL

Created by Glenna Goodacre, this tribute to the women who served in Vietnam, most of them nurses, was dedicated in 1993. Of the more than 58,000 names inscribed upon the Wall, eight are women, which is also the number of trees present in the sculpture's grove. Goodacre noted that she wanted this image of a soldier being saved by three women "to be a monument for the living."

THE THREE SERVICEMEN

This bronze sculpture, created by Frederic Hart, was dedicated in 1984, two years after the creation of the Wall Memorial. It was added as a compromise after critics complained the Wall was too abstract and lacked a heroic, life-like depiction of an American soldier.

In preparation for his work, Hart interviewed dozens of veterans and watched film footage and documentaries from the war, stating, "The contrast between the innocence of their youth and the weapons of war underscores the poignancy of their sacrifice. There is about them the physical contact and sense of unity that bespeaks the bonds of love and sacrifice that is the nature of men at war... Their strength and their vulnerability are both evident."

Vietnam War Memorial

Vietnam War Memorial

Military Women's Memorial

Honoring the service of women in the United States Armed Forces is the Military Women's Memorial, located on the grounds of Arlington National Cemetery. Following Congressional approval for the memorial in 1985, organizers sought an existing location for its site, believing that to be a more suitable option than trying to secure space on the National Mall. Their search led them to Arlington, where an aging building sat in a state of disrepair, virtually unused.

The Hemicycle, a semi-circular building built in 1932, was originally designed to serve as a ceremonial entrance for Arlington National Cemetery. With a commitment to restore the Hemicycle to serve as the home for the Women's Memorial, a revised design plan created by Michael Manfredi, Marion Weiss and Associates was approved in 1992.

Following two years of construction, the memorial was dedicated on October 18, 1997 and features computer terminals where visitors can search a vast database for women who have served in the U.S. Armed Forces from the Revolutionary War to the War in Afghanistan. Stairs leading to the top of the Hemicycle also offer views of Memorial Avenue and the surrounding cemetery, with quotations inscribed in a number of skylights that also provide a view of the interior below.

WOMEN IN MILITARY SERVICE FOR AMERICA MEMORIAL

This Memorial honors the women who have served in and with the US Armed Forces from the time of the American Revolution to the present. Although women did not officially serve in the military until the 20th century, many women served with the military in earlier times of crisis.

MILITARY WOMEN'S MEMORIAL - *Housed in the Hemicycle, the semi-circular shaped building pictured above, the Military Women's Memorial offers two recessed stairways leading visitors upward to enjoy views of Memorial Avenue and thought-provoking quotes inscribed on skylights. At a focal point of the Memorial, located at the center of the Hemicycle, is a fountain with 200 jets of water that empty into a pool some 80 feet in diameter.*

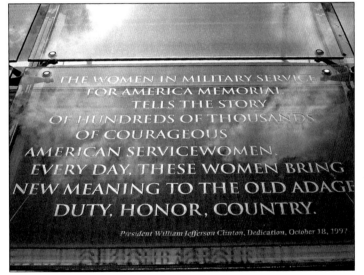

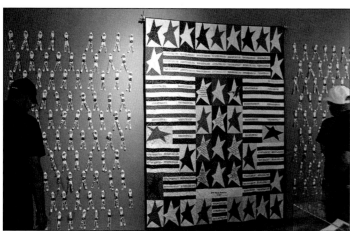

Thank You for Your Service

Cedar Valley
Honor Flight
Sullivan ★ Hartogh ★ Davis
Waterloo
Waterloo, Iowa

On growing up in a military family:

"My mom was [also] in the army and she never let my dad forget that she outranked him!"

~Sue Gress, Honor Flight Organizer

Military Women's Memorial

Arlington National Cemetery

Silence and Respect

The origin of Arlington National Cemetery has a rich history dating back to the earliest years of the United States of America. Established by George Washington's adopted grandson, George Washington Parke Custis, Arlington House was initially designed to serve as a living memorial to the nation's first president.

When Custis died in 1857, he willed the estate to his daughter, Mary Custis Lee, who had married Robert E. Lee in 1831. The terms of the will specified that Mrs. Lee would own the estate for the duration of her life, where, upon her death, it would then be passed on to her eldest son.

Though Robert E. Lee served as the executor of his father-in-law's will, he never actually owned the property.

When the Civil War broke out, the Lees abandoned the property in 1861. On May 24, 1861, the United States Army seized Arlington Estate for its strategic value; the elevated landscape would serve as home to three forts built there during the war.

The first military burial at Arlington was held on May 13, 1864 for Private William Christman. At that time, Brigadier General Montgomery Meigs, who was responsible for the burial of soldiers, ordered Arlington Estate to be used as a cemetery, because two

existing national cemeteries in the Washington, D.C. area, Soldiers' Home Cemetery and Alexandria National Cemetery, were running out of space.

By order of Secretary of War, Edwin Stanton, Arlington officially became a national cemetery on June 15, 1864. It was originally 200 acres in size. It has since grown to be more than 630 acres, with over 400,000 veterans and their eligible dependents buried there.

On November 11, 1921, the Tomb of the Unknown Soldier was dedicated, with interment of the Unknown from World War I.

On November 25, 1963, President John F. Kennedy became the second U.S. president to be buried at Arlington. William Howard Taft was the first.

Following President Kennedy's televised state funeral, requests for burial at Arlington spiked for many years. To prevent the cemetery from running out of space, the U.S. government established new regulations to restrict in-ground burials while authorizing expansion for additional space.

Arlington National Cemetery

Arlington National Cemetery

CHANGING OF THE GUARD

There can be no doubt that one of the highlights of any Honor Flight is a visit to Arlington National Cemetery to witness the Changing of the Guard Ceremony.

Since 1948, soldiers from the 3rd U.S. Infantry Regiment, known as "The Old Guard," have been entrusted to stand watch over the Tomb of the Unknown Soldier. They do so 24 hours a day, regardless of weather conditions. The qualifications to become a Sentinel, or Tomb Guard, are so demanding that only a very small percentage of those who apply for this prestigious post are successful in achieving this special assignment.

The ceremony begins shortly after the relief commander, in full dress uniform, appears on the plaza, followed by a new Sentinel who makes the walk from the quarters located below the Memorial Display Room. When the new Sentinel unlocks the bolt of his/her M-14 rifle, the relief commander walks out to the Tomb, often making a distinctive scraping sound with the heel of a shoe as a sign of respect when Honor Flight veterans are present. After saluting the Tomb, the relief commander then turns to address the spectators. It is requested (and expected) that all in attendance remain silent and standing during the ceremony.

The relief commander first conducts a very detailed, white glove inspection of the new Sentinel's rifle, followed by a close review of the Sentinel's uniform. When finished, the pair join the retiring Sentinel at the center of the black mat in front of the Tomb, where all three salute the three unknown soldiers buried there.

"Pass on your orders," the relief commander then states to the relieved Sentinel.

"Post and orders, remain as directed," the Sentinel replies.

The new Sentinel acknowledges the orders by stating, "Orders acknowledged," then takes his/her position on the mat. All three then salute the Tomb one more time before the retiring Sentinel exits, followed by the relief commander.

Nearly every action a Sentinel takes while guarding the Tomb is tied to the highest military honor that can be bestowed, the 21-gun salute. The Tomb guard marches exactly 21 steps on the black mat before turning to face east for 21 seconds, then north for 21 more seconds. Then it's another 21 steps back down the mat before repeating the process all over again.

Arlington National Cemetery

Arlington National Cemetery

Arlington National Cemetery

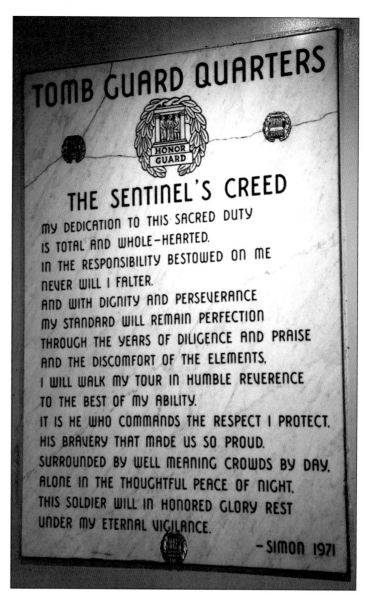

TOMB GUARD QUARTERS

HONOR GUARD

THE SENTINEL'S CREED

MY DEDICATION TO THIS SACRED DUTY
IS TOTAL AND WHOLE-HEARTED.
IN THE RESPONSIBILITY BESTOWED ON ME
NEVER WILL I FALTER.
AND WITH DIGNITY AND PERSEVERANCE
MY STANDARD WILL REMAIN PERFECTION
THROUGH THE YEARS OF DILIGENCE AND PRAISE
AND THE DISCOMFORT OF THE ELEMENTS.
I WILL WALK MY TOUR IN HUMBLE REVERENCE
TO THE BEST OF MY ABILITY.
IT IS HE WHO COMMANDS THE RESPECT I PROTECT.
HIS BRAVERY THAT MADE US SO PROUD.
SURROUNDED BY WELL MEANING CROWDS BY DAY,
ALONE IN THE THOUGHTFUL PEACE OF NIGHT,
THIS SOLDIER WILL IN HONORED GLORY REST
UNDER MY ETERNAL VIGILANCE.

— SIMON 1971

WREATH LAYING CEREMONY

WREATH LAYING CEREMONIES - *Cedar Valley Honor Flight has had the honor of participating in multiple wreath laying ceremonies at Arlington National Cemetery. The first (above) occurred on September 22, 2015 and included Ed McFarland, Dick Backes, Niki Rinaldi and Linda Bergmann. Nearly a year later (below), Cedar Valley Honor Flight veterans Roger Clemons, Clayton Ohrt, Terry Bean and Ron Black participated in a wreath laying ceremony held on September 13, 2016.*

Thank You for Your Service

Waterloo, Iowa

On laying a wreath at the Tomb of the Unknowns Soldiers:

"It was very solemn and very, very humbling to be able to recognize the unknown soldiers and to show homage to the rest of the veterans that were in attendance."

~Ed McFarland, Honor Flight Organizer

SPACE SHUTTLE CHALLENGER - On January 28, 1986, Space Shuttle Challenger exploded 73 seconds after takeoff, killing all seven crew members: Commander Michael J. Smith; Commander Francis R. 'Dick' Scobee; Ronald E. McNair, mission specialist; Ellison Onizuka, mission specialist; S. Christa McAuliffe, payload specialist and America's first teacher in space; Gregory B. Jarvis, payload specialist; Judith A. Resnik, mission specialist. On May 20, 1986, the comingled cremated remains of the seven Challenger astronauts were buried at Arlington National Cemetery, in Section 46, Grave 1129. Located near the Memorial Amphitheater, a dedication ceremony commemorating the marker was held on March 21, 1987.

SPACE SHUTTLE COLUMBIA - Following a 16-day scientific mission on February 1, 2003, Space Shuttle Columbia burst into flames and disintegrated as it re-entered the Earth's atmosphere, killing all seven crew members aboard: Richard "Rick" Husband, commander; William C. McCool, pilot; Michael P. Anderson, payload commander; David M. Brown, mission specialist; Kalpana Chawla, mission specialist; Laurel Blair Salton Clark, mission specialist; and Ilan Ramon, mission specialist. Dedicated on February 2, 2004, the marker is adjacent to the Challenger Memorial and features the names of the astronauts as part of a silhouette of the space shuttle, surrounded by seven stars.

IRAN RESCUE MISSION - This Memorial commemorates the role of U.S. service members during an aborted mission to rescue 66 American hostages during the Iranian Revolution of 1979, in which eight service personnel were killed. Iran did not release the hostages until January 20, 1981, after they had been held for nearly fifteen months of additional captivity. Dedicated in 1983, the Iran Rescue Mission Memorial consists of a white marble column with a bronze plaque listing the names and ranks of those who lost their lives during the mission. It is located in Section 46 of Arlington National Cemetery near the Challenger and Columbia Space Shuttle Memorials.

AUDIE MURPHY GRAVE SITE - *One of the most decorated soldiers or World War II, Audie Murphy was wounded three times and earned 28 medals, all before his 21st birthday. Murphy's grave site is also located near the Memorial Amphitheater, making it a popular destination for Cedar Valley Honor Flight veterans to pay their respects.*

"REMEMBER THE MAINE"

MAINE MAST MEMORIAL - Commissioned in 1895, *Maine* was the first U.S. Navy ship to be named after the state of Maine. Classified as an armored cruiser or second-class battleship, *Maine* was sent to Havana Harbor to protect American interests during the Cuban War of Independence. On February 15, 1898, an explosion ripped open the ship's hull, killing more than 260 sailors, roughly three quarters of the crew. Twelve years after the ship sank, the Army Corps of Engineers raised the *Maine* and, in 1912, transferred its mast to Arlington. On May 30, 1915, President Woodrow Wilson dedicated the Memorial after the *Maine's* mast was mounted on a granite base, designed to represent the turret of a battleship. Welded into the door of the base is the *Maine's* bell, with an inscription that reads: "USS MAINE, Navy Yard, New York, 1894." Above the door that leads into the base, another inscription reads: "Erected in memory of the officers and men who lost their lives in the destruction of the *USS Maine* at Havana Cuba, February Fifteenth MDCCCXCVIII."

Arlington National Cemetery

Arlington National Cemetery

ARLINGTON NATIONAL CEMETERY'S MEMORIAL AMPHITHEATER - *A visit to the Memorial Amphitheater near Memorial Day is an especially stunning sight to see. Dedicated on May 15, 1920, the amphitheater replaced Arlington National Cemetery's original amphitheater, now known as the James R. Tanner Amphitheater, which could no longer accommodate the large crowds that official ceremonies attracted. Designed by Thomas Hastings, the colonnaded building consists primarily of Vermont-quarried Danby marble. Its interior spaces include a Memorial Chapel and Memorial Display Room, which features exhibits on the history of Arlington National Cemetery and the Tomb of the Unknown Soldier. Inscriptions above the colonnade list 44 major battles fought by the U.S. military, from the American Revolution to the Spanish-American War.*

Arlington National Cemetery

Arlington National Cemetery

United States Marine Corps Memorial

On February 23, 1945, Marines of Company E, 2nd Battalion were tasked with the challenge of scaling and capturing Mount Suribachi on the small island of Iwo Jima. By 10:30 that morning, their success was evident when a small American flag could be seen waving at the top of the 550 foot peak. That afternoon, when the area had been cleared of resistance, a second, larger flag was raised. After Associated Press photographer Joe Rosenthal captured the image that would later earn him a Pulitzer Prize, sculptor Felix W. de Weldon, who had enlisted in the U.S. Navy, constructed a scale model of the image.

At the conclusion of World War II, Congress commissioned deWeldon to create a statue for the Marine Corps Memorial based on the famous photograph that the U.S. Navy was able to determine depicted Corporal Harlon Block, Corporal Harold P. Keller, Private First Class Ira Hayes, Private First Class Harold Schultz, Private First Class Franklin Sousley and Sergeant Michael Strank. When deWeldon completed the statue in plaster, it was trucked in pieces to Brooklyn, New York, where it was cast in bronze, a process that took three years. The various pieces were then hauled to Washington, D.C., where they were assembled and treated with preservatives.

On November 10, 1954, President Dwight D. Eisenhower dedicated the memorial on the 179th anniversary of the U.S. Marine Corps.

At the base of the statue, which stands about 78 feet tall, the names and dates of every principal U.S. Marine Corps engagement is rimmed in gold. The imposing size of the memorial depicts soldiers that are 32 feet tall, raising a 60 foot flag pole. The rifles are 16 and 12 feet long, respectively. The canteen, if functional, would hold 32 quarts of water.

Thanks to a 1961 presidential proclamation, the flag flies at full mast 24 hours a day.

The entire cost of the statue ($850,000) was donated by the U.S. Marine Corps, friends of the Marine Corps and members of the Naval Service.

Driving around the memorial in a counter-clockwise direction creates the optical illusion of the flag being raised.

70,000 Marines Helped Raise That Flag on Iwo Jima

"...to Marines it's not about the individuals and never has been....what they did together and what they represent remains most important. That doesn't change."

—General Robert B. Neller
USMC Commandant, 2016

If you have only seen the famous photo that inspired this statue, you might get the impression that just six Marines got the whole job done. But there were several photographers at work that day—and many other photos made.

Here you can see a part of the actual Marine combat patrol that took the Stars and Stripes up Mount Suribachi, past snipers concealed in the sides of that volcano. Some of these faces are here in the war memorial statue.

What you can't see is the great armada of 500 ships and swarms of warplanes that made it possible to put three Marine divisions and an Army regiment ashore—more than 110,000 sailors, airmen, soldiers, and Marines.

Many of the faces in this combat patrol photo would die on Iwo in the bitter fighting in the weeks to come. The sacrifices made to win Iwo Jima were greater than any other battle in Marine Corps history.

NETHERLANDS CARILLON:
A gift symbolizing Dutch-American friendship, on April 4, 1952, the Netherlands' Queen Juliana presented a small bell to President Harry S. Truman as a token for the carillon to come, a gift from the people of the Netherlands to the United States. Initially installed at West Potomac Park two years later, a permanent tower was eventually built adjacent to the Marine Corps Memorial. On May 5, 1960, the fifteenth anniversary of the liberation of the Netherlands from the Nazis, a dedication ceremony of the carillon was held. Two subsequent renovations have been made to the carillon: In 1995 in honor of the 50th anniversary of the liberation of the Netherlands, and in 2022 the addition of three more bells made it a Grand Carillon consisting of a total of 53 bells.

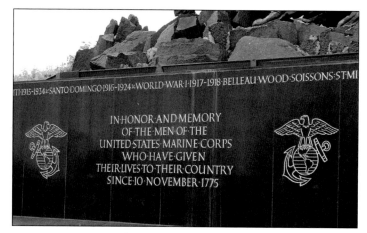

3ᵏFRENCH·NAVAL·WAR·1798-1801 ⅄ TRIPOLI·1801-1805 ⅄ WAR·OF·1812-1815 ⅄ FLORIDA·INDIAN·WARS·1835

United States Air Force Memorial

INTO THE WILD BLUE YONDER

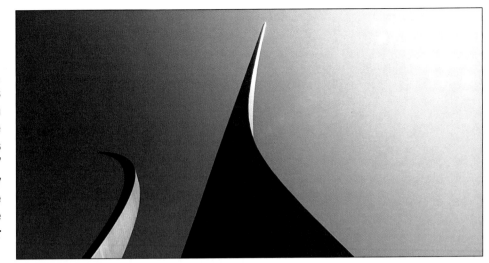

The United States Air Force Memorial, dedicated on October 14, 1996, features three stainless-steel spires, ranging in height from 201 to 270 feet tall, to symbolize the "contrails of the Air Force Thunderbirds as they peel back in a precision 'bomb burst' maneuver." As the Thunderbirds typically fly in a formation of four planes, the absence of a fourth spire is thought to symbolize the missing man formation flown during Air Force funeral flyovers.

Located at the east end of Columbia Pike, on the grounds of Fort Myer, just south of Arlington National Cemetery, the memorial was designed by James Ingo Freed.

Two inscription walls, one each at the north and south ends, stand 10 feet high and 56 feet in length. The north wall contains the names of Air Force recipients of the Medal of Honor, while the south wall has inspirational quotations related to the Air Force's three core values: "integrity first, service before self, and excellence in all we do."

Standing before the south wall are four bronze statues representing an Air Force Honor Guard, where a close inspection reveals one of the "airmen" is actually female. The four 8-foot tall bronze statues were sculpted by Zenos Frudakis.

In front of the north wall is a free-standing glass panel with the images of four F-16s flying in a missing man formation.

USAF Memorial

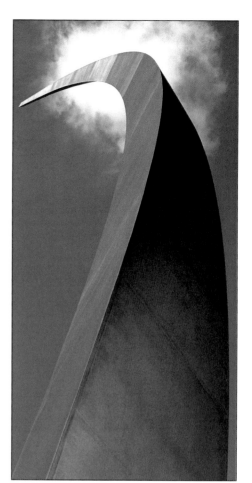

USAF Memorial

MISSING MAN FORMATION: A FINAL SALUTE TO A FALLEN COMRADE

THE HERITAGE OF
THE UNITED STATES AIR FORCE
AND ITS COMBAT CAMPAIGNS

AERONAUTICAL DIVISION OF THE U.S. ARMY SIGNAL CORPS
CREATED AUGUST 1, 1907

AVIATION SECTION OF THE U.S. ARMY SIGNAL CORPS
CREATED JULY 18, 1914

WWI
Mexican Expedition Campaign: March 14, 1916 - February 7, 1917
Somme Defensive: March 21 - April 6, 1918
Lys: April 9 - 27, 1918

DIVISION OF MILITARY AERONAUTICS, SECRETARY OF WAR
CREATED MAY 20, 1918

U.S. ARMY AIR SERVICE
CREATED MAY 24, 1918
WWI
Champagne-Marne: July 15 - 18, 1918
Aisne-Marne: July 18 - August 6, 1918
Somme Offensive: August 8 - November 11, 1918
Oise-Aisne: August 18 - November 11, 1918
St. Mihiel: September 12 - 16, 1918
Meuse-Argonne: September 26 - November 11, 1918

U.S. ARMY AIR CORPS
CREATED JULY 2, 1926

INTEGRITY   SERVICE   EXCELLENCE

INTEGRITY
INTEGRITY FIRST

Integrity; a man's word is his bond.

GENERAL JIMMY DOOLITTLE
U.S. Army Air Forces, leader of the WWII Tokyo Raid

*Integrity is the fundamental premise of service in a free society.
Without integrity, the moral pillars of our military strength –
public trust and self-respect are lost.*

GENERAL CHARLES A. GABRIEL
Eleventh Chief of Staff, United States Air Force

*We're entrusted with the security of our nation. The tools of our
trade are lethal, and we engage in operations that involve risk
to human life and untold national treasure. Because of what we do
our standards must be higher than those of society at large.*

GENERAL RONALD R. FOGLEMAN
Fifteenth Chief of Staff, United States Air Force

*There will be demands upon your ability, upon your endurance,
upon your disposition, upon your patience...Just as fire tempers iron
into fine steel so does adversity temper one's character
into firmness, tolerance and determination.*

SENATOR MARGARET CHASE SMITH
Lt Colonel, United States Air Force Reserve

SERVICE
SERVICE BEFORE SELF

*I have been recognized as a hero for ten minutes
of action over Vietnam, but I am no more a hero than anyone
else who has served their country.*

A1C JOHN L. LEVITOW
Lowest Ranking Airman Medal of Honor Recipient

*Service is a willingness to sacrifice...the setting aside
of personal desires, comfort, and security when the safety of
the country is at stake.*

GENERAL GEORGE S. BROWN
Eighth Chief of Staff, United States Air Force &
Eighth Chairman, Joint Chiefs of Staff

*Service before self is that virtue within us all which elevates
the human spirit; compels us to reach beyond our meager selves
to attach our spirit to something bigger than we are.*

GENERAL JOHN P. JUMPER
Seventeenth Chief of Staff, United States Air Force

EXCELLENCE
EXCELLENCE IN ALL WE DO

*The future is always decided by those who put
their imagination to work, who challenge the unknown,
and who are not afraid to risk failure.*

GENERAL BERNARD A. SCHRIEVER
The Father and Architect of Air Force Space and Ballistic Missile Programs

*The power of excellence is overwhelming. It is always in demand
and nobody cares about its color.*

GENERAL DANIEL 'CHAPPIE' JAMES
First African-American United States Air Force Four-Star General

*That commitment to excellence is more than desirable;
in the profession of arms, it's essential. Lives depend on the fact
that we maintain high standards.*

GENERAL MICHAEL E. RYAN
Sixteenth Chief of Staff, United States Air Force

*Courage and innovation form our heritage and excellence is
our standard. America's Airmen - Active, Guard, and Reserve -
serve as a force unmatched in air and space.*

GENERAL T. MICHAEL 'BUZZ' MOSELEY
Eighteenth Chief of Staff, United States Air Force

CELEBRATING 25 FLIGHTS - *Board members traveling with veterans on Cedar Valley Honor Flight's 25th flight from Waterloo, Iowa on September 10, 2019 (from left): Janet Schupbach, Linda Bergmann, David Grimm, Frank Magsamen and Niki Rinaldi.*

Franklin Delano Roosevelt Memorial

Cedar Valley Honor Flight's 28th trip to Washington, DC in 2022 included two new stops on the itinerary, the first being the Franklin Delano Roosevelt Memorial. Designed by architect Laurence Halprin, construction of the 7.5 acre memorial began on September 16, 1991. The completed project was dedicated on May 2, 1997 and consists of five outdoor rooms that represent each of President Roosevelt's four terms in office, plus a prologue (added in 2001). The memorial contains 31,269 granite stones, the largest weighing 4.5 tons. Over 100,000 gallons of water flows in seven fountains and ponds.

In his book The Franklin Delano Roosevelt Memorial, Halprin stated, "In the FDR Memorial, I hoped to evoke as many emotions as I could. I wanted the experience of this Memorial to reveal the dramatic story that unfolded during President Roosevelt's four terms, the twelve years when he was President of the United States. His was a hero's journey- from the urgency of his first term of office and the New Deal, through his struggles to overcome the Great Depression, through the trauma of World War II, and finally to his search for an honorable and lasting peace."

The Prologue Room features a life-sized sculpture of FDR, diagnosed with polio at the age of 39, sitting in a wheelchair. Each of the successive rooms depict critical issues the nation faced during each of his terms in office.

Room One features a waterfall that was constructed to reflect the president's simple and direct messages to the country.

Room Two uses a sculpture of men waiting in a free bread line to help illustrate the Great Depression, while another sculpture of a man sitting by a radio depicts the fireside chats that Roosevelt used to communicate directly with the American people.

World War II dominates the contents of Room Three, with scattered granite blocks illustrating the destruction of war.

President Roosevelt died of a stroke just a few months into his fourth term in 1945. Room Four contains a low-relief panel featuring his funeral procession, as well as a statue of his wife, First Lady Eleanor, who helped create the United Nations Declaration of Human Rights following FDR's death.

> MEN AND NATURE MUST WORK
> HAND IN HAND. THE THROWING
> OUT OF BALANCE OF THE RESOURCES
> OF NATURE THROWS OUT OF
> BALANCE ALSO THE LIVES OF MEN.

FRANKLIN DELANO ROOSEVELT MEMORIAL

> THE TEST OF OUR PROGRESS
> IS NOT WHETHER WE ADD MORE
> TO THE ABUNDANCE OF THOSE
> WHO HAVE MUCH; IT IS WHETHER
> WE PROVIDE ENOUGH FOR
> THOSE WHO HAVE TOO LITTLE.

FDR Memorial

WE MUST SCRUPULOUSLY
GUARD THE CIVIL RIGHTS
AND CIVIL LIBERTIES OF
ALL CITIZENS, WHATEVER
THEIR BACKGROUND.
WE MUST REMEMBER THAT
ANY OPPRESSION, ANY
INJUSTICE, ANY HATRED, IS
A WEDGE DESIGNED TO
ATTACK OUR CIVILIZATION

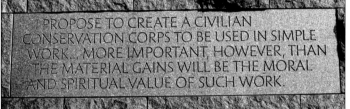

I PROPOSE TO CREATE A CIVILIAN
CONSERVATION CORPS TO BE USED IN SIMPLE
WORK... MORE IMPORTANT, HOWEVER, THAN
THE MATERIAL GAINS WILL BE THE MORAL
AND SPIRITUAL VALUE OF SUCH WORK.

ELEANOR ROOSEVELT
FIRST UNITED STATES DELEGATE
TO THE UNITED NATIONS

UNLESS THE PEACE THAT FOLLOWS RECOGNIZES
THAT THE WHOLE WORLD IS ONE NEIGHBORHOOD
AND DOES JUSTICE TO THE WHOLE HUMAN RACE,
THE GERMS OF ANOTHER WORLD WAR WILL
REMAIN AS A CONSTANT THREAT TO MANKIND.

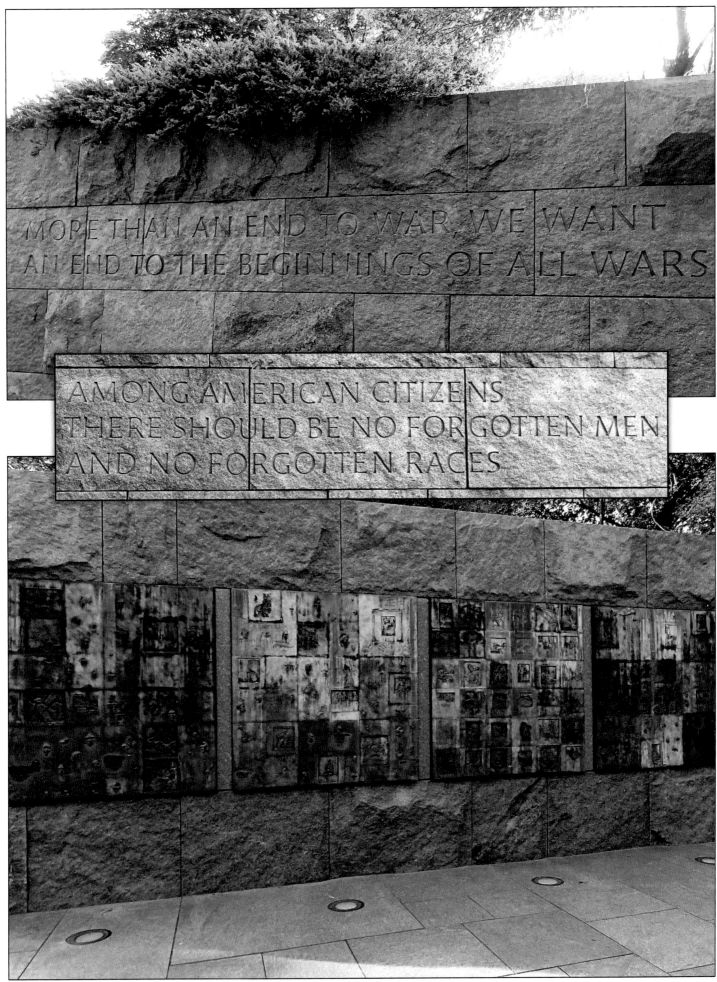

MORE THAN AN END TO WAR, WE WANT
AN END TO THE BEGINNINGS OF ALL WARS

AMONG AMERICAN CITIZENS
THERE SHOULD BE NO FORGOTTEN MEN
AND NO FORGOTTEN RACES

1945 / FOURTH TERM
"He Died in Harness"

Voters did not know the seriousness of Franklin Roosevelt's heart disease when they elected him to a fourth presidential term. With victory in sight, FDR made a final trip to Eastern Europe and the Middle East. At Yalta, he negotiated post-war agreements with the Soviet Union and Great Britain. On his return, Roosevelt addressed Congress seated, saying, "It makes it a lot easier for me not to have to carry about ten pounds of steel around on the bottom of my legs." He died months before the end of World War II.

This bas relief (right) by sculptor Leonard Baskin represents a grieving nation. Baskin placed a riderless, blanket-draped horse honoring the fallen commander at the head of the procession. Mourners with heads bowed walk behind the casket.

FDR died on April 12, 1945. New President Harry Truman told reporters he felt as though "the moon, the stars, and all the planets had fallen on me." A horse-drawn caisson transported Roosevelt's body through Washington, D.C., from Union Station to the White House.

"More than an end to war, we want an end to the beginnings of all wars."
Undelivered Address
Prepared for April 13, 1945

MEMORIAL QUOTES IN ROOM FOUR

"Unless the justice that follows recognizes that the whole world is one neighborhood and does justice to the whole human race, the germs of another world war will remain as a constant threat to mankind."
Radio Address, February 12, 1943

THE FUNERAL CORTEGE — HORSE WITH FLAG — CAISSON WITH FDR'S COFFIN — MOURNERS

WE HAVE FAITH THAT FUTURE GENERATIONS WILL KNOW THAT HERE, IN THE MIDDLE OF THE TWENTIETH CENTURY, THERE CAME A TIME WHEN MEN OF GOOD WILL FOUND A WAY TO UNITE, AND PRODUCE, AND FIGHT TO DESTROY THE FORCES OF IGNORANCE, AND INTOLERANCE, AND SLAVERY, AND WAR.

Martin Luther King, Jr. Memorial

Also new to the Cedar Valley Honor Flight itinerary in 2022 was a visit to the Martin Luther King, Jr. Memorial. Following Dr. King's assassination in 1968, the Phi Alpha Phi fraternity, of whom King became a member while completing his doctoral studies at Boston University in the early 1950s, proposed erecting a monument in his honor in Washington, D.C.. The proposal garnered more attention in 1986, the first year King's birthday was celebrated as a national holiday in the United States.

In 1996, the United States Congress authorized the Secretary of the Interior to permit Alpha Phi Alpha to establish a memorial, giving the fraternity until 2003 to raise $100 million and break ground. A ceremonial ground-breaking for the memorial was held on November 13, 2006, in West Potomac Park. Actual construction of the memorial began in December 2009, with it being opened to the public on August 22, 2011.

Designed by ROMA Design Group, the memorial's address, 1964 Independence Avenue, references the 1964 Civil Rights Act.

The central focus of the memorial is based on a phrase from the "I Have a Dream" speech Martin Luther King, Jr. delivered at the Lincoln Memorial on August 28, 1963; "Out of a mountain of despair, a stone of hope." A 30 foot high relief of Dr. King, carved in granite, is aptly named the "Stone of Hope," which stands past two other pieces of granite visitors pass through known as the "Mountain of Despair."

The placement of the Stone of Hope is designed to give the impression that King is looking toward the horizon over the Tidal Basin.

The inclusion of cherry trees on the site allow them to bloom each year during the anniversary of his death, which occurred on April 4, 1968.

The remainder of the memorial features a 450 foot long inscription wall, with famous quotes from many of his speeches engraved into a crescent-shaped granite wall.

MARTIN LUTHER KING, JR. MEMORIAL

EVERY NATION MUST NOW DEVELOP AN OVERRIDING LOYALTY TO
MANKIND AS A WHOLE IN ORDER TO PRESERVE THE
BEST IN THEIR INDIVIDUAL SOCIETIES.

THE ULTIMATE MEASURE OF A MAN IS NOT WHERE HE STANDS
IN MOMENTS OF COMFORT AND CONVENIENCE,
BUT WHERE HE STANDS AT TIMES OF
CHALLENGE AND CONTROVERSY.

1963

IT IS NOT ENOUGH TO SAY, "WE MUST NOT WAGE WAR." IT IS NECESSARY TO
LOVE PEACE AND SACRIFICE FOR IT. WE MUST CONCENTRATE NOT
MERELY ON THE NEGATIVE EXPULSION OF WAR, BUT ON
THE POSITIVE AFFIRMATION OF PEACE.

CALIFORNIA, 1967

I HAVE THE AUDACITY TO BELIEVE THAT PEOPLES EVERYWHERE CAN
HAVE THREE MEALS A DAY FOR THEIR BODIES, EDUCATION AND
CULTURE FOR THEIR MINDS, AND DIGNITY, EQUALITY,
AND FREEDOM FOR THEIR SPIRITS.

NORWAY, 1964

MLK Memorial

The Veterans

During the earliest Cedar Valley Honor Flight trips to the nation's capital, attempts to gather the nearly 100 men and women spilling out of three tour buses for a group photo proved challenging. It soon became clear that no one photo of such a large group could do justice to the many faces included in the portrait. After mixed results with photographs taken at the World War II Memorial and the U.S. Marine Corps Memorial, someone had the great idea that taking group photos by tour bus was the best way to feature each veteran in attendance. Grouping veterans by their red, white and blue bus designations made taking the group photos faster and easier to manage, while also allowing guardians an excellent opportunity to take their own photos of the veterans with whom they shared an unforgettable day in Washington, D.C..

With nearly 3,000 area veterans served by Cedar Valley Honor Flight, not every veteran who has made the trip originating from Waterloo, Iowa appears on the following pages. However, the faces pictured here vividly illustrate the many reasons why a committed group of volunteers have spent years working diligently to honor them for their service.

The Veterans

The Veterans

The Veterans

The Veterans

The Veterans

The Veterans

The Veterans

The Veterans

The Veterans

The Veterans

The Veterans

The Veterans

Welcome Home

YOU'VE GOT MAIL
(AND A VISIT FROM MISS MARYLAND)

What could be better than a full day of sights and sounds in Washington, D.C.? On more than one occasion, Cedar Valley Honor Flight veterans were greeted by the reigning Miss Maryland at the airport, who was there to see them off before their flight home.

And the flight home comes with yet another surprise- a special care package courtesy of Mail Call, a bundle of letters from family members, friends and area schoolchildren, thanking the veterans for their service.

Upon arrival back home in Waterloo, the veterans are given a first class welcome home, serenaded by the Cedar Valley Big Band and hundreds of cheering people who show their support with signs, handshakes and hugs.

CEDAR VALLEY BIG BAND

For more than 30 years, the Cedar Valley Big Band has been performing throughout Eastern Iowa, a group of musicians donating their talents to promote jazz and the love of music for listeners of all ages. Their presence at the Waterloo Regional Airport, along with featured vocalist Felicia Smith Nall, entertains the throng of people who gather there, eager to welcome the Cedar Valley Honor Flight veterans home. And when the veterans finally make their way into the terminal, the sounds of the Cedar Valley Big Band performing such standards as "American Patrol," "In the Mood" and "Sing, Sing, Sing" really help make the welcome home celebration an unforgettable experience.

Thank You for Your Service

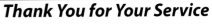

Cedar Valley
Sullivan ★ Hartogh ★ Davis
Honor Flight
Waterloo

Waterloo, Iowa

On serving Cedar Valley veterans:
"We can do anything for these guys-anything. One time I said, 'If you want me to stand on my head, I'll practice, but I'm not real good at it now.' We [really do] try to accommodate"
~Linda Bergmann, Honor Flight Organizer

Welcome Home

Welcome Home

Welcome Home

Welcome Home

Welcome Home

Thank You for Your Service

Sullivan ★ Hartogh ★ Davis
Cedar Valley
Honor Flight
Waterloo

Waterloo, Iowa

On the welcome home at the Waterloo Regional Airport:

"A lot of people coming back, they don't [expect it]. They're just totally in awe when they come in and that airport is packed. It's the welcome home they never got, especially for the Vietnam veterans."

~*Lee Bedore, Honor Flight Organizer*

Welcome Home

Welcome Home

Acknowledgements

There would be no photographic journey without photographs. My thanks to photographers Jane Whittlesey, Mary Bauer, John Klotzbach and Katie Davison for beautifully illustrating the intent of the Honor Flight program with the images they have captured over the years. I am also grateful for the time Cedar Valley Honor Flight volunteers spent with me sharing their own personal stories to help readers better understand the motivation behind the mission. While there are so many contributors who have helped Cedar Valley Honor Flight provide unforgettable experiences for thousands of Iowa veterans, special thanks go to Craig White, Frank Magsamen, Linda Bergmann, Lee Bedore, David Cole, Sue Gress, Dave Grimm, Janet Liming, Ed McFarland, Burk Miehe, Barb O'Rourke, Barry Remington, Janet Schupbach and Teresa Schmitz.

About the Author

Mike's love for reading and writing began at an early age, spurred on by Library Media Specialist Rita Wilson while attending elementary school at Travis Air Force Base. His introduction to journalism came as a freshman in high school, where he began to learn the skills of news writing and graphic design that would serve him well in later years.

Following high school, Mike earned a Bachelor's Degree in Elementary Education at Mount Mercy College and a Master's Degree in Library and Information Management from Emporia State University, before working as a teacher, technology facilitator and elementary school principal.

In 2002, Mike and his wife, Jane, bought their hometown newspaper, *The Progress Review*. As Editor and Publisher, Mike and his staff earned dozens of state awards over the next 18 years, building a reputation as one of the top small-town newspapers in the state of Iowa.

He and his wife live in La Porte City, Iowa, where they are constantly entertained by three cats (Alegria, Gracie and Chloe) and a dog (Chica Sue).

Best of Cedar Valley Honor Flight DVD

"You're gonna see some stuff that's gonna make you go 'Ooh and aah!'"

So said Mr. G., a tour bus driver, to Cedar Valley Honor Flight veterans at the beginning of an eventful day in Washington, D.C..

Relive some of the best moments from Cedar Valley Honor Flights with this special DVD featuring 120 minutes of video footage. Scan the code below or logon to www.palmertownpress.com to order your DVD for just $9.95, plus shipping and handling. Proceeds from the sale of each "Best Of" DVD benefit Cedar Valley Honor Flight.

THE BEST OF

Sullivan ★ Hartogh ★ Davis
Cedar Valley
Honor Flight
Waterloo

Waterloo, Iowa

THE MONUMENTS, MEMORIALS AND MORE

Each DVD includes the following programs:

PRE-FLIGHT MEETING
At a June 2013 pre-flight meeting, Craig White tells the origin story of Cedar Valley Honor Flight. Randy Miller and Dan McGowan present the Table of Honor. Running Time - 14:45

OH YAY! OH YAY! OH YAY!
During the Sept. 13, 2016 Honor Flight, a town crier greets the veterans upon their arrival in Baltimore. Running Time - 0:23

WELCOME TO BALTIMORE: WATER SALUTE
The May 24, 2016 Honor Flight is met with a water cannon salute. Bus driver Mr. G. explains Washington, D.C.. Running Time - 3:07

WELCOME TO BALTIMORE: GEN. PURSER
Bob Lowe and Major General Leslie A. Purser welcome the May 29, 2017 Honor Flight veterans to Baltimore. Running Time - 3:19

WORLD WAR II WALK-AROUND TOUR
Shot during the May 11, 2022 Honor Flight, this video features a walking tour of the World War II Memorial. Running Time - 16:32

LESSONS FROM BOB THE TOUR GUIDE
An Honor Flight tour guide provides educational background about the World War II, Lincoln, Korean War and Vietnam War memorials to veterans during the May 7, 2019 Honor Flight. Running Time - 13:33

MARINE SILENT DRILL PLATOON
The "Marching 24," a platoon of Marines, perform at the Lincoln Memorial during the May 11, 2022 Honor Flight. Running Time - 7:02

WREATH LAYING CEREMONY
Cedar Valley Honor Flight helps conduct a wreath laying ceremony on Sept. 22, 2015. Running Time - 7:40

CHANGING OF THE GUARD
Veterans aboard the Sept. 10, 2019 Honor Flight witness the Changing of the Guard ceremony. Running Time - 8:53

IWO JIMA
On the May 7, 2019 Honor Flight, a drive around of the U.S. Marine Corps Memorial illustrates the optical illusion of the flag being raised. Running Time - 0:37

FAREWELL FROM BALTIMORE: MISS MARYLAND
Veterans aboard the May 9, 2017 Honor Flight join Miss Maryland for a rendition of "God Bless America." Running Time - 4:10

Made in the USA
Monee, IL
10 March 2024

54215323R00100